At Issue

Cancer

Other Books in the At Issue Series:

At Issue

Cancer

Belinda Mooney, Book Editor

GREENHAVEN PRESS
An imprint of Thomson Gale, a part of The Thomson Corporation

Detroit • New York • San Francisco • New Haven, Conn. • Waterville, Maine • London

Christine Nasso, *Publisher*
Elizabeth Des Chenes, *Managing Editor*

© 2007 Thomson Gale, a part of The Thomson Corporation.

Thomson and Star logo are trademarks and Gale and Greenhaven Press are registered trademarks used herein under license.

For more information, contact:
Greenhaven Press
27500 Drake Rd.
Farmington Hills, MI 48331-3535
Or you can visit our Internet site at http://www.gale.com

Articles in Greenhaven Press anthologies are often edited for length to meet page requirements. In addition, original titles of these works are changed to clearly present the main thesis and to explicitly indicate the author's opinion. Every effort is made to ensure that Greenhaven Press accurately reflects the original intent of the authors. Every effort has been made to trace the owners of copyrighted material.

Cover photograph reproduced by permission of Tom Stewart/CORBIS.

ISBN-13: 978-0-7377-3411-9 (lib. : alk. paper)
ISBN-10: 0-7377-3411-6 (lib. : alk. paper)
ISBN-13: 978-0-7377-3412-6 (pbk. : alk. paper)
ISBN-10: 0-7377-3412-4 (pbk. : alk. paper)

Library of Congress Control Number: 2006938251

Printed in the United States of America
10 9 8 7 6 5 4 3 2 1

Contents

Introduction

According to the American Cancer Society, approximately 1.4 million Americans will be diagnosed with cancer in 2006, and altogether some 10.5 million Americans alive today have had a cancer diagnosis at some time in their lives. In 2006 nearly 550,000 people will die of cancer, which is second only to heart disease as the leading cause of death in the United States. Nevertheless, there is good news in the battle against cancer. According to official figures published in October 2006 in the "Annual Report to the Nation on the Status of Cancer, 1975–2003," Americans' risk of dying from cancer has been steadily declining since the early 1990s. This overall long-term decline applies to both sexes and all races, but the greatest drop in death rates has occurred in men: From 1993 to 2003, a drop of 1.6 percent per year, double the decline of 0.8 percent per year in women. Somewhat paradoxically, however, the overall incidence of cancer—that is, the rate at which new cancers are diagnosed—has been stable over this period, and rates of diagnosis have actually increased for women.

Two important factors explain this apparent contradiction. First, intense efforts to reduce smoking have significantly reduced deaths from lung cancer. Adult smoking has dropped dramatically since the 1960s, and though youth smoking rates rose during much of the 1990s, youth smoking too has declined since 1997. As Betsy A. Kohler, president of the North American Association of Central Cancer Registries, notes:

> The greater decline in cancer death rates among men is due in large part to their substantial decrease in tobacco use. We need to enhance efforts to reduce tobacco use in women so that the rate of decline in cancer death rates becomes comparable to that of men.

Second, improved screening programs mean more cancers are detected earlier in their development, with two results:

Less advanced cancers are easier to treat and have better survival rates, so cancer patients live longer; but the more people undergo screening tests the more diagnoses are made, actually increasing the overall incidence of cancer.

A closer look at statistics shows specific increasing and decreasing trends. Among women, for example, the incidence of cancer has decreased for colon and rectal cancers: uterine, ovarian, and cervical cancers (attributed to widespread screening tests such as annual PAP tests), and oral and stomach cancers. Significantly, the death rates from breast, prostate, lung, and colorectal cancers—the four most common kinds of cancer—have all dropped. This good news has been attributed to reducing a variety of risk factors in addition to screening tests such as mammograms and the reduction in smoking. For example, more people are reducing alcohol and fat consumption and slightly increasing fruit and vegetable consumption, and more people are doing more to reduce their exposure to direct sunlight, whose ultraviolet rays are a known cause of skin cancer.

Since 1975, however, the incidence of non-Hodgkin lymphoma, melanoma, leukemia, and cancers of the lungs, thyroid, bladder, and kidney has increased in women. The incidence of prostate and testicular cancer and cancers of the pancreas, kidney, liver, and esophagus has risen in men, and overall incidence of childhood cancer has risen slightly. Experts suggest that in addition to improved screening programs, lifestyle factors play a role in these increases as well: More Americans are overweight or obese, for example, and overall levels of physical exercise have changed very little since the 1980s.

One of the most notable findings of the "Annual Report to the Nation" is the unexplained differences in cancer incidence among population subgroups, specifically the higher rates of both cancer incidence and cancer deaths among blacks and Hispanics/Latinos. The cancer-related mortality rate for African American women, for example, is 28 percent higher than that for white women. The U.S. Latino population, the most rapidly growing ethnic group in the nation, is more likely than non-Hispanic whites to suffer from several cancers that have known infectious origins: human papilloma virus (HPV) in cervical cancer, *Helicobacter pylori* in stomach cancer, and hepatitis B and hepatitis C in liver cancer. And Latino children have a higher incidence of leukemia, retinoblastoma, and the bone cancer osteosarcoma than non-Latino white children.

Some analysts have pointed to socioeconomic factors as the cause of these disparities. A larger percentage of African Americans and Hispanics fall into low-income brackets and live in poorer communities, which has been linked to higher exposure to environmental risk factors in neighborhoods and workplaces; lower education and health awareness, and thus less likelihood of seeking health-care services or screening programs; and less access to health care often due to lack of health insurance. Genetic predisposition to certain cancers may be a factor as well, among all population groups, and is the focus of ongoing research.

Today cancer is understood as not a single disease but a category of diseases with widely varying causes, courses, and outcomes, and undeniably high social and medical costs. *At Issue: Cancer* examines the many factors involved in the causes and treatment of cancer. Until a cure for cancer is found, debates surrounding cancer treatment and prevention will likely remain heated and emotional.

Secondhand Smoke Causes Cancer

Katrina Woznicki

Katrina Woznicki is a journalist in Edgewater, New Jersey, and writes frequently about women's health issues.

A new study indicates that second hand smoke causes cervical cancer in women. The peer-reviewed study indicates that women who are exposed to secondhand smoke are more likely to develop cervical cancer. Other research shows that minorities, in particular are at a greater risk to develop cervical cancer when second hand smoke is a factor. The best way to combat these new findings is to enact public smoking bans and increase education.

Women exposed to secondhand smoke increase their risk of developing cervical cancer, according to a [current] study from Johns Hopkins Bloomberg School of Public Health.

The study published in the January [2005] issue of *Obstetrics and Gynecology* could have critical health implications as public health advocates work to not only educate women about reducing their risks for cervical cancer, but also lower tobacco use around the globe.

There Is Strong Convicting Evidence

"The evidence is strong," said lead researcher Anthony J. Alberg, an assistant professor in the department of epidemiology. "The findings should encourage smokers to quit and warn nonsmokers who live with smokers to decrease their secondhand smoke exposure."

While researchers have long suspected that secondhand smoke raised cervical cancer rates, the study—one of the big-

Katrina Woznicki, "Cervical Cancer Tied to Secondhand Smoke," *Women's Enews*, January 25, 2005. www.womensenews.org/article.cfm/dyn/aid/2160/context/archive. Reproduced by permission.

gest in the United States—makes the link more definitive. The results are being seen as especially important for women living in developing countries, where smoking is on the rise and cervical cancer is a leading cause of death.

Alberg and his team examined the exposures of 51,173 women age 25 and older in Washington County, Md., to household smoking in 1963 and then 1975. The women filled out questionnaires about their exposure to cigarette smoke, who currently or formerly smoked in their households, household member ages, years of education and marital status. Each group was followed 15 years. Researchers then compared women who lived with nonsmokers to women who lived with smokers and monitored who developed cervical cancer.

Investigators found that women exposed to passive smoking faced a 2.1-fold increased risk for the disease in 1963. By [the] 1975 study group, that figure dropped to a 1.4-fold greater risk.

Alberg said he was "puzzled" by this drop and had "no clear explanation for it." He speculated that one possible reason was that the women in the 1975 group were working outside of the home and may have reduced their household exposure to tobacco.

Passive Smoking Is Linked to Cancer

William Au, professor in the department of preventive medicine and community health at the University of Texas Medical Branch in Galveston, Texas, said the study, which was peer-reviewed, proves a conclusive link.

"This is a well-conducted study based on scientific protocol and it has tremendous implications to human health," he said. "We're now seeing how low levels of toxic substances such as secondhand smoke can cause cancer in the human population."

Passive smoking has been known to increase the risks for heart disease and lung cancer in both men and women, and active cigarette smoking has been long established as a major risk factor for cervical cancer. Although scientists have suspected a link between secondhand smoke and cervical cancer, they needed more data to prove it.

It is really important [that] people get the message that smoking does much more than we ever thought that it did.

Risk of Cancer Not Trivial

One of the more recent studies came from Singapore and was published in the April [2004] issue of *Gynecologic Oncology*. Researchers studied 623 women and found their risk of certain abnormal cervical cells that signal the possible onset of cervical cancer increased by 4.6 percent for every cigarette the woman's spouse smoked.

"At this point it is difficult to discern the extent to which secondhand smoke exposure contributes to the population rates of cervical cancer," Alberg said, "but our findings and the fact that exposure to secondhand smoke is common suggest the contribution of secondhand smoke exposure may not be trivial."

"It's really important [that] people get the message that smoking does much more than we ever thought that it did and that it affects our health in ways we don't even fully know about yet," said Hollis Forster, executive director of the National Cervical Cancer Coalition, a nonprofit organization in Berkeley, Calif.

Special Risks for Minorities

Twenty-two percent of the U.S. population smoked in 2003, down from 24 percent in 1998, according to the federal Centers for Disease Control and Prevention. The American Cancer Society reports there are more than 10,000 cases of invasive cervical cancer every year in the United States and the disease claims 3,900 lives. In the United States, African American women are most vulnerable to cervical cancer, according to the Atlanta-based Centers for Disease Control and Prevention.

The Centers for Disease Control reports [that] from 1992–2000, only 62.6 percent of African American women survived cervical cancer five years after being diagnosed compared to a survival rate of 73.3 percent among white women. The federal agency also reports higher Pap smear testing, the gold standard of screening for cervical cancer, among white women.

While smoking rates have been dropping steadily in this country and cervical cancer rates have followed suit thanks to detection with Pap smear tests—a gynecological screening of cervical mucus for abnormal cells—the rates for both remain a serious public health threat elsewhere around the world.

In developing nations, cervical cancer is the second-leading cause of cancer deaths among women after lung cancer, with 80 percent of the 500,000 new cases every year occurring in Latin America, Africa, and Southeast Asia.

Although easily treated if detected, cervical cancer remains a top public health threat because of HPV, human papillomavirus, a sexually transmitted infection that causes the disease. Scientists around the globe are racing to develop a vaccine to block HPV infection.

Alberg said he suspects tobacco exposure may exacerbate HPV infection. "It is possible that cigarette smoke acts in concert with HPV to promote progression to cancer," Alberg said.

Impaired Immune System

Smoking of any kind, direct or passive, can impair the immune system making it vulnerable to infection, including HPV, said Au. Carcinogens found in tobacco smoke "cause DNA damage or gene mutation" and can block cells' abilities to repair themselves, Au said.

Women, however, should not think being around cigarette smoke will directly result in HPV infection. While smoking is unrelated to the acquisition of HPV infection, it is "related to immunity, which is important in the progression" of cervical tumors, said Janet Daling, an investigator at the Fred Hutchinson Cancer Research Center in Seattle.

More Public Bans on Smoking Are Needed

The rising number of public smoking bans may make it easier for women in the United States to protect themselves, but such safeguards against public exposure to secondhand smoke are few and far between elsewhere in the world.

"The banning of smoking in public places is just the beginning," said Au. "First, it's the ban. Second, it's education. We don't want people to quit smoking in public places and then just smoke in the home. That puts family members and children at risk."

There Is No Convincing Evidence That Secondhand Smoke Causes Cancer

Donald B. Louria

Donald B. Louria is the editor of the Healthful Life E-valuator *online newsletter.*

Secondhand smoke may bother some people, but it is nothing more than an annoyance. Despite arguments linking secondhand smoke to cancer, there is very little evidence to actually back up these arguments. In fact, many experts agree that studies and findings related to secondhand smoke have been inadequate, if not flawed. Until anti-smoking advocates have substantial and reliable evidence that there is a clear link between secondhand smoke and cancer, they should stop perpetuating this myth.

Inhaling the cigarette smoke of others can be very annoying. Second-hand smoke can also increase the frequency of bronchitis and other respiratory infections in children, and it activates asthma and bronchitis. There is no argument about those unpleasant and unhealthy consequences of passive smoking. It is the following other claims that create controversy:

- that passive smoking increases the risk of coronary heart disease and heart attacks by 25 percent.

- that passive smoking can increase the risk of lung cancer in non-smokers by several fold; but, lung cancer is infrequent in non-smokers so that translates to only a 17 to 22 percent increase in risk.

Donald B. Louria, "Passive Smoking: The Debate Explodes," Healthful Life Project, June 2003. http://healthfullife.umdnj.edu/archives/passive_smoke_archive.htm. Reproduced by permission.

- that passive smoking causes 3,000 lung cancer cases a year (out of a total of about 170,000 cases each year in the United States). That figure was sort of picked out of the hat; it is not really based on any adequate data.

The supposed increased risk of heart attacks or lung cancer is actually quite small—in this type of study, an increase of 17 to 25 percent is not very much. At least partly on the basis of these alleged risks, public anti-smoking policy in restaurants and bars has been established with bombastic statements about how many lives would be saved by these new anti-smoking regulations relating to second-hand smoke.

Exposure to environmental tobacco smoke was not significantly associated with the death rate for . . . lung cancer.

There have always been well-respected doubters. In January 2002, we reviewed several interesting reports that questioned whether passive smoking really did cause any increase in heart attacks and lung cancer. . . .

That is the setting for a report in May 2003 in the *British Medical Journal* by James Enstrom of the School of Public Health, University of California in Los Angeles, and Geoffrey Kabat of the Department of Preventive Medicine, State University of New York at Stony Brook. Their study is titled "Environmental Tobacco Smoke and Tobacco-Related Mortality in a Prospective Study of Californians 1960-98." They studied 35,561 individuals who were never smokers, but had a smoking spouse. Their main (and controversial) finding was "exposure to environmental tobacco smoke was not significantly associated with the death rate for coronary heart disease (heart attacks), lung cancer, or chronic obstructive pulmonary disease in men or women."

The response was ferocious.

Study Causes Outrage Among Experts

The study was called "inadequate," "flawed," "inaccurate," "unreliable," "biased." Commented one highly-respected epidemiologist, "we have one very flawed study that does not find an association. It flies in the face of so much evidence and so much scientific understanding that it just doesn't contribute."

The American Cancer Society had institutional apoplexy. One spokesperson even challenged the study because some of the funding came from tobacco companies.

What goes on here? James Enstrom is no crackpot; he is a highly-respected epidemiologist who has carried out many good studies, including studies on the long-term dangers of smoking.

In responding to the intemperate attacks, Enstrom said "maybe the feelings about this issue are so strong that no one cares what the evidence shows."

We still do not know whether passive (second-hand) smoke causes an increased frequency of . . . lung cancer.

Let's be clear. There is nothing wrong with this study—it is thoughtfully and carefully conducted.

There Is Still Serious Doubt

The bottom line is that, as of this writing . . . we still do not know whether passive (second-hand) smoke causes an increased frequency of coronary heart disease, heart attacks, or lung cancer.

Cigarette smoking causes plenty of problems for smokers. It causes some problems for non-smokers, especially children and those with asthma or bronchitis. And, it can be annoying to non-smokers or those sensitive to the smoke. BUT, it has not been shown persuasively to cause either lung cancer or heart attacks. Anti-smoking enthusiasts should stop using claims about heart attacks or lung cancer in their campaigns until such time, if ever, that we have persuasive supporting evidence.

Sun Exposure Increases the Risk of Cancer

Cleveland Clinic Health Information Center

The Cleveland Clinic Health Information Center strives to provide current information on important health topics.

Sunbathing and other exposure to the sun will not only cause wrinkles and age spots, but can also lead to more serious conditions such as skin cancer. Although family history and skin type do play a part in contributing to the likelihood of skin cancer, the risks of overexposure to the sun apply equally to everyone. There is no way to undo sun damage, but you can decrease your risk of further damage by using sunscreen every day and staying out of the sun.

Many people love the sun. The sun's rays make us feel good, and in the short term, it makes us look good. But our love affair isn't a two way street: Exposure to sun causes most of the wrinkles and age spots on our faces. Consider this: One woman at age 40 who has protected her skin from the sun actually has the skin of a 30-year-old.

We often associate a glowing complexion with good health, but skin color obtained from being in the sun can actually mean accelerated effects of aging and an increased risk for developing skin cancer.

Sun exposure causes most of the skin changes that we think of as a normal part of aging. Over time, the sun's ultraviolet (UV) light damages the fibers in the skin called elastin. When these fibers breakdown, the skin begins to sag, stretch, and lose its ability to go back into place after stretching. The

Cleveland Clinic Health Information Center, "Sun Exposure and Skin Cancer," 2003. www.clevelandclinic.org/health/health-info/docs/3100/3163.asp?index=10985. Reproduced by permission.

skin also bruises and tears more easily—taking longer to heal. So while sun damage to the skin may not be apparent when you're young, it will definitely show later in life.

Skin cancer is the most prevalent form of all cancers in the U.S.

Skin Cancer May Be Lurking

Skin cancer is the most prevalent form of all cancers in the U.S. and the number of cases continues to rise. It is the uncontrolled growth of abnormal skin cells. While healthy cells grow and divide in an orderly way, cancer cells grow and divide in a rapid, haphazard manner. This rapid growth results in tumors that are either benign (noncancerous) or malignant (cancerous).

There are three main types of skin cancer: basal cell carcinoma, squamous cell carcinoma, and melanoma. Basal cell and squamous cell cancers are less serious types and make up 95 percent of all skin cancers. Also referred to as non-melanoma skin cancers, they are highly curable when treated early.

Melanoma, made up of abnormal skin pigment cells called melanocytes, is the most serious form of skin cancer and causes 75 percent of all skin cancer deaths. Left untreated, it can spread to other organs and is difficult to control.

The Causes of Skin Cancer

Ultraviolet (UV) radiation from the sun is the number one cause of skin cancer, but UV light from tanning beds is just as harmful. Exposure to sunlight during the winter months puts you at the same risk as exposure during the summertime.

Cumulative sun exposure causes mainly basal cell and squamous cell skin cancer, while episodes of severe sunburns, usually before age 18, can cause melanoma later in life. Other less common causes are repeated X-ray exposure, scars from burns or disease, and occupational exposure to certain chemicals.

The risk is greatest for people who have fair or freckled skin that burns easily.

Some People Have Higher Risk

Although anyone can get skin cancer, the risk is greatest for people who have fair or freckled skin that burns easily, light eyes and blond or red hair. Darker skinned individuals are also susceptible to all types of skin cancer, although their risk is substantially lower.

Aside from complexion, other risk factors include having a family history or personal history of skin cancer, having an outdoor job and living in a sunny climate. A history of severe sunburns and an abundance of large and irregularly-shaped moles are risk factors unique to melanoma.

Signs and Symptoms of Skin Cancer

The most common warning sign of skin cancer is a change on the skin, typically a new mole or skin lesion or a change in an existing mole.

- Basal cell carcinoma may appear as a small, smooth, pearly or waxy bump on the face, ears and neck; or as a flat, pink/red- or brown-colored lesion on the trunk or arms and legs.

- Squamous cell carcinoma can appear as a firm, red nodule, or as a rough, scaly flat lesion that may itch, bleed, and become crusty. Both basal cell and squamous cell cancers mainly occur on areas of the skin frequently exposed to the sun, but can occur anywhere.

- Melanoma usually appears as a pigmented patch or bump. It may resemble a normal mole, but usually has a more irregular appearance.

When looking for melanoma, think of the ABCD rule that tells you the signs to watch for:

- Asymmetry—the shape of one half doesn't match the other

- Border—edges are ragged or blurred

- Color—uneven shades of brown, black, tan, red, white or blue

- Diameter—A significant change in size (greater than 6 mm)

Diagnosis and Treatment

Skin cancer is diagnosed only by performing a biopsy. This involves taking a sample of the tissue, which is then placed under a microscope and examined by a dermatopathologist, or doctor who specializes in examining skin cells. Sometimes a biopsy can remove all of the cancer tissue and no further treatment is needed.

Treatment of skin cancer depends on the type and extent of the disease. Treatment is individualized and is determined by the type of skin cancer, its size and location and the patient's preference.

Standard treatments for non-melanoma skin cancer (basal cell or squamous cell carcinomas) include:

- Mohs surgery (for high-risk non-melanoma skin cancers)—excision of cancer and some extra tissue

- Electrodesiccation and curettage—physically scraping away the skin cancer cells followed by electrosurgery

- Cryosurgery or freezing

- Laser therapy

- Drugs (chemotherapy, biological response modifiers to destroy cancer cells)

Standard treatments for melanoma skin cancer include:

- Wide surgical excision

- Sentinel lymph node mapping (for deeper lesions)—to determine if the melanoma has spread to local lymph nodes

- Drugs (chemotherapy, biological response modifiers)

- Radiation therapy

- New methods in clinical trials are sometimes used to treat skin cancer.

Preventing Skin Cancer

Nothing can completely undo sun damage, although the skin can sometimes repair itself. So, it's never too late to begin protecting yourself from the sun. Your skin does change with age—for example, you sweat less and your skin can take longer to heal, but you can delay these changes by staying out of the sun.

Sun Exposure Actually Reduces the Risk of Cancer

Nan Kathryn Fuchs

Nan Kathryn Fuchs is the author of the best sellers The Nutrition Detective: A Woman's Guide to Treating Your Health Problems Through the Foods You Eat, Overcoming the Legacy of Overeating, *and* User's Guide to Calcium and Magnesium *and is the editor and writer of* Womens's Health Letter, *the leading health advisory on nutritional healing for women.*

Despite what many doctors advise, sun exposure is not always harmful. In fact, exposure to the sun is necessary to protect you from disease. Doctors that advocate for liberal use of sunscreen, even for short-term exposure, are ignoring the fact that chemicals used in sunscreen can be far more damaging than sunlight. Sunlight is a great source of vitamin D that should be embraced through moderate exposure.

There's a nutrient your body can produce with a little outside help that can protect you from cancer, diabetes, depression, and osteoporosis. It's low in people with autoimmune diseases, such as multiple sclerosis, rheumatoid arthritis, and Crohn's disease.

A Necessary Nutrient Produced by the Sun

Doctors of integrative medicine are prescribing it in large doses to their patients for all of these conditions and are finding it beneficial. What's more, it's readily available. You can walk into any health food store and get it in supplement form, or you can get it for absolutely nothing.

Nan Kathryn Fuchs, "Avoiding the Sun? Sunlight Actually Prevents Cancers," *Women's Health Letter*, vol. 11, April 2005, pp. 4–6. Copyright © 2005 by Soundview Communications, Inc. All rights reserved. Reproduced by permission.

Unfortunately, your doctor may be scaring you away from taking advantage of this free solution to so many devastating diseases.

What is it? Vitamin D, the sunshine vitamin. If you spend enough time outdoors, the sunlight will help your body make vitamin D.

This, in turn, can reduce your risk for a host of health problems.

[Doctors] say that any exposure to the sun's ultraviolet (UV) rays promotes cancers. This is only half true.

Telling a Half Truth

But dermatologists and other doctors are saying that sunlight, the foundation for all life on this planet, is dangerous. They're telling you to slather your body with sunscreen before you leave the house to go shopping or spend a little time in the garden. They say that any exposure to the sun's ultraviolet (UV) rays promotes cancers. This is only half true. Unlike man-made radiation (which is unsafe at any level), UV rays are harmful only in excessive amounts. In small doses, researcher William Grant, PhD, found that UVB radiation [a type of ultraviolet radiation] actually protects against 16 forms of cancer.

It's been said that UV exposure increases your risk for non-Hodgkin's lymphoma (NHL), a group of cancers that begin in the lymph cells. But a 60-year-long study from Australia found the opposite was true. Exposure to the sun actually protected people from NHL. Those with the most exposure to sunlight had a 35 percent lower risk for getting these cancers than people with the least. What about those who only spent time outdoors on weekends and holidays? They had less than half the risk for NHL over people who remained indoors.

Sunlight and Skin Cancers

What about skin cancers? It's true that too much sunlight can be dangerous. It's not smart to spend hours every day in intense sun. It's not healthy to get sunburns. In fact, the more you burn—especially when you're young—the more likely you are to end up with skin cancers. But knowing this shouldn't prevent you from spending some time outdoors in the sun, getting your daily dose of vitamin D.

The most dangerous form of skin cancer is melanoma. Everyone I've met who has had a melanoma is afraid to get any sun on their skin. Yet a 10-year study of sailors in the Navy found that sailors who worked indoors had more melanomas than those who worked both indoors and outdoors. What's even more surprising is that there were more melanomas on their midsections than on their exposed faces or arms.

Deciding How Much Sun

How much sunlight is enough and not too much? It depends on whom you ask. Traditional doctors say that you can get around 400 IU of vitamin D a day by exposing your face and arms to 15 minutes of light a day. They say this is enough. I don't agree. It may be enough to prevent rickets and other vitamin D-deficiency diseases, but it won't give you the same protection as 15–30 minutes of exposure to very bright sunlight each day.

The time of day you're in the sun determines how much vitamin D your body can make. Dr. Grant points out that we can't convert vitamin D from UVB radiation unless the sun is high in the sky. So get outside for 15–30 minutes before or after lunch each day. If you go outdoors at other times, you'll need a longer exposure. During the winter, the sun isn't high enough or close enough for your body to make vitamin D from sunlight. That's when you need to rely on supplements.

Four hundred IU a day is the bare minimum. But you may need to begin with up to 10,000 IU for a short time to raise depleted levels. If you haven't been getting much sunlight, ask your doctor to test you for vitamin D deficiency with a test called 25-hydroxyvitamin D—or 25(OH)D. Then have him or her monitor your levels as you take large doses.

The Problem with Sunscreens

A lot of [sunscreens] are filled with junk-chemicals that promote the production of dangerous free radicals and chemicals with estrogenic [creating female hormones] effects. In fact, most of these ingredients are banned in Europe. Only buy products with titanium dioxide or zinc oxide. They're safe and effective. You can find them in health food stores and some pharmacies.

Sunscreens won't work if they have less than SP-15 protection or if they're out of date. Check the expiration date on your sunscreen and replace it if it's old.

Sunlight is your ally, not your enemy.

Diet Aids Sunlight in Cancer Prevention

Antioxidants in your diet protect your skin from becoming damaged by UV radiation and from nonmelanoma skin cancers. These include carotenoids (vitamin A), tocopherols (vitamin E), ascorbate (vitamin C), flavonoids, and omega-3 fats (fish oil, flax oil). Include plenty of fresh fruits and vegetables in your diet.

In Norway, where there's little sunlight during the winter months, vitamin D deficiency is common. More than two dozen Norwegians were given a diet high in fatty fish and cod liver oil—all high in vitamin D. In fact, the participants were given more than 54 times the recommended daily requirements. All of the people who continued eating diets high in vitamin D were able to sustain sufficient vitamin D in their blood throughout the winter.

Sunlight Is Your Ally

Sunlight is your ally, not your enemy. Be smart. Get outdoors and increase your vitamin D. For more information on sunlight, vitamin D, and cancers, read some of the articles by cancer researcher Ralph Moss, PhD, at www.cancerdecisions .com.

Australians have been warned about the effects of sunlight in increasing skin cancers for more than a decade. As a result, they tend to stay out of the sun. Now a significant number of Australians have been found to have a vitamin D deficiency. The key is to get moderate exposure to bright sunlight. And use the right sunscreen.

Pesticides Increase the Risk of Cancer

Journal of Environmental Health

The Journal of Environmental Health *is a published by the National Environmental Health Association.*

A new study of agricultural pesticides shows that some pesticides can be linked to certain types of cancer. Findings indicate that workers who handle these pesticides and have a family history of cancer have the highest risk for developing cancer, and that minorities are also at an increased risk. In addition, the study shows a link between prostate cancer in farmers and workers and certain pesticides.

Exposure to certain agricultural pesticides may be associated with an increased risk of prostate cancer among pesticide applicators, according to a large study looking at the causes of cancer and other diseases in the farming community. The study, part of a long-term study of pesticide applicators and their spouses known as the Agricultural Health Study (AHS), appears in the May 1, 2003, issue of the *American Journal of Epidemiology*. The AHS is a collaborative effort involving the National Cancer Institute (NCI), the National Institute of Environmental Health Sciences, and the Environmental Protection Agency.

The latest report from the AHS evaluates the role of 45 pesticides and found that only a few of them showed evidence of a possible association with prostate cancer among pesticide applicators. Methyl bromide was linked to the risk of prostate cancer in the entire group, while exposure to six other pesticides was associated with an increased risk of prostate cancer only among men with a family history of the disease.

Agricultural Workers at Greatest Risk

"Associations between pesticide use and prostate cancer risk among the farm population have been seen in previous studies; farming is the most consistent occupational risk factor for prostate cancer," said Michael Alavanja, Dr.P.H., from NCI's Division of Cancer Epidemiology and Genetics in Bethesda, Maryland, and principal investigator of the AHS.

The AHS, which began in 1993, is following nearly 90,000 participants from North Carolina and Iowa over time to evaluate the role of a variety of agricultural and lifestyle exposures on health. The participants are either farmers, wives of farmers, or workers who use pesticides on a regular basis.

The risk of developing prostate cancer was 14 percent greater for the pesticide applicators than for the general population.

The current study included 55,332 men who are classified as either "private pesticide applicators" (92 percent) or "commercial pesticide applicators" (8 percent). Private applicators are farmers or nursery-workers. Commercial applicators work for pest control companies or for businesses such as warehouses or grain mills that use pesticides regularly. Between 1993 and 1999, 566 new prostate cancers developed among all applicators, compared to 495 that were predicted from the incidence rates in the two states. This means that the risk of developing prostate cancer was 14 percent greater for the pesticide applicators than for the general population. The men in this study were followed for about 4.3 years.

Methyl Bromide Is Carcinogenic

Methyl bromide is a fumigant gas used nationally to protect crops from pests in the soil and to fumigate grain bins and other agricultural storage areas. The scientists found that among both North Carolina and Iowa pesticide applicators, the risk of prostate cancer rose with increasing frequency of use of methyl bromide and with longer lifetime exposure to this pesticide. Elevated risks were seen only at the two highest levels of exposure (out of five possible levels). Risks were two to four times higher than among men who were not exposed to methyl bromide. Based on animal studies, the National Institute for Occupational Safety and Health (NIOSH) lists methyl bromide as a potential occupational carcinogen.

"We cannot rule out the possibility that our observation occurred by chance alone," cautioned Aaron Blair, Ph.D. M.P.H., chief of the Occupational and Environmental Epidemiology Branch in NCI's Division of Cancer Epidemiology and Genetics and an author of the current study. "Clearly, these findings need to be replicated. But, the internal consistency of our findings does not allow us to dismiss these results."

More Links to Pesticides

The researchers found another link between pesticides and prostate cancer: Among men with a family history of prostate cancer, exposure to six pesticides—chlorpyrifos, coumaphos, fonofos, phorate, permethrin, and butylate—was associated with an increased risk of prostate cancer. This effect was not seen among those without a family history. This type of finding, i.e., something appearing in only a subgroup of the entire study population, is particularly difficult to interpret, since it could result from chance or from differences between subgroups other than their use of pesticides. However, four of these pesticides, chlorpyrifos, coumaphos, fonofos, and phorate, are thiophosphates and share a common chemical structure. These findings suggest that certain pesticides may interact with a particular form of one or more genes shared by men with a family history of prostate cancer, making them more susceptible to developing the disease.

The most consistent risk factors associated with prostate cancer are age, family history, and African-American ethnicity. Hormonal factors and high levels of animal fat and red meat in the diet are also suspected risk factors. Several previous occupational studies have linked farming to prostate cancer risk. However, the variety of environmental exposures in the farming community such as pesticides, engine exhausts, solvents, dusts, animal viruses, fertilizers, fuels, and specific microbes, have made it difficult for researchers in previous studies to sort out which of these factors is linked to specific diseases. Because of the large size of the AHS population, and the detailed information on specific exposures and risk factors collected by the AHS researchers, it is possible to evaluate the risks associated with a number of specific chemical exposures.

As the study continues and participants age, many new cases of cancer and other diseases will develop. With time, the researchers will be able to confirm or refute the current findings, assess additional relationships between exposures and diseases, and search for possible genetic links to the variety of environmental exposures in the farming community.

Pesticides Do Not Cause Cancer in Humans

PestFacts.org

PestFacts.org is a Web site designed to educate the public about pesticides and their use.

Although some pesticides have been linked to cancer in laboratory animals, low levels of these substances will not cause cancer in humans. Pesticides help protect the environment and food sources. They do not raise the risk of cancer in humans.

A pesticide is any natural or synthetic substance that can be used to control or kill pests of any sort, including insects, fungi, rodents, and weeds. There are a few specific pesticides that have been shown to cause cancer in laboratory rodents. Pesticides do not cause cancer in people. In 1997, a panel of international cancer experts evaluated over seventy published studies. "The Panel concluded that it was not aware of any definitive evidence to suggest that synthetic pesticides contribute significantly to overall cancer mortality."

Environmental Levels Do Not Cause Cancer

Population studies and studies of the harmful properties of synthetic pesticides and other industrial chemicals do not support a cause-and-effect relationship between exposure to low levels of these materials and cancer.

Pesticide exposure is only one of many potential causes being investigated. To be able to say with confidence that no association exists between pesticides and childhood cancer, the potential for such an association must be thoroughly studied. Many of the studies looking at these questions have been un-

PestFacts.org, "Pesticides and Cancer Q&A," February 2006. www.pestfacts.org/qa/cancer.html. Reproduced by permission.

derway since the late 1980s. . . . Other potential environmental causes of cancer being investigated include infectious agents, maternal diet during pregnancy, ultraviolet and ionizing radiation, certain medications, food additives, tobacco, alcohol, heavy metals and air pollution.

Pesticide Residue on Foods

Federal and state governments regulate pesticides. These regulations require the compounds to go through over 120 separate tests before they can be registered for use, and their safety continues to be monitored. Foods continue to be tested when they are taken from the fields and from the grocery market basket. . . . A panel of cancer experts including members of the American Cancer Society concluded in 1997 that a diet rich in fruits and vegetables is important in the reduction of cancer risk.

Sexually Transmitted Diseases Increase the Risk of Cancer

Planned Parenthood

Planned Parenthood provides education and services on repro-ductive issues.

The causes of cancer are constantly being evaluated and debated. It is now known that sexually transmitted diseases (STDs) such as the HPV virus are present in most types of cervical and other reproductive organ cancers. STDs also contribute to other types of cancer.

It is estimated that in 2006 there will be about 9,710 new cases of invasive cervical cancer in the United States, which will result in about 3,700 deaths (ACS, 2006a). Worldwide, nearly 500,000 new cases are diagnosed each year (WHO, 2005). Cervical cancer is the second most common type of cancer among women worldwide and one of the leading causes of cancer–related mortality in women in the developing world (WHO, 2006). The median age of diagnossis for cervical cancer for all races is 48 years (Ries, et al., 2006). Half of all women diagnosed with cervical cancer are between the age of 35 and 55 (ACS, 2006a).

Cervical Cancer Is a Strong Threat

Due largely to routine screening using Pap tests, the number of deaths attributed to cervical cancer in the United States dropped 74 percent between 1955 and 1992, and the death rate contiues to drop nearly four percent annually (ACS, 2006a). The five–year survival rate is virtually 100 percent for pre–invasive cervical cancer, and 91 percent for early invasive cancer. The overall five–year survival rate for all stages of cervical cancer is about 73 percent (ACS, 2006a).

African–Americans experience a disproportionate number of deaths from cervical cancer—due mainly to underscreeening in this population. In 2001, the death rate was 4.7 per 100,000 for black women, compared to 2.2 per 100,000 for white women (Ries, et al., 2005). Latinas and Native Americans also have cervical cancer death rates that are above average (NCI, 2005).

Large studies have found that HPV is present in more than 99 percent of cervical cancer tumors.

Cervical Cancer May Be Sexually Transmitted

Since the late 1800s, researchers have suspected that cervical cancer was sexually transmitted. Medical reports noted that nuns and virgins were not likely to have cervical cancer, and that women who were married to men who traveled a great deal or who had previous wives who died of cervical cancer were more likely to develop cervical cancer ("The Cervical Cancer Virus," 1995). Today, 15–20 types of HPV have been classified as oncogenic, and the DHHS [Department of Health and Human Services] has added HPV to the list of cancer–causing agents (Janicek & Averette, 2001; Kay, 2005; Munoz, et al., 2003; Schiffman & Castle, 2003; Wiley, et al., 2002). Large studies have found that HPV is present in more than 99 percent of cervical cancer tumors (Clifford, et al., 2003; Walboomers, et al., 1999). HPV 16 and 18 are responsible for about 70 percent of all cervical cancers. Other HPV types are associated with the remaining 30 percent of cases (Bosch & deSanjosé, 2003; Clifford, 2003; Shah, 1997).

Most HPV infections never lead to the development of cervical cancer—even in the absence of medical intervention—and appropriate management of precancerous cervical lesions detected by Pap tests has greatly reduced the rate of invasive cervical cancer (Ho, et al., 1998; NCI, 1999a). Only one out of 1,000 women with HPV develops invasive cervical cancer (ACOG, 2000).

HPV Necessary to Cervical Cancer

HPV appears to be necessary, but not sufficient, to the development of cervical cancer. Besides HPV type, researchers believe there are several cofactors that may contribute to the development of cervical cancer. These may include alcohol consumption, smoking, diet, familial history, HIV infection, hormonal factors—including multiple pregnancies and the use of both oral contraceptives and DES, low socioeconomic status, the presence of other sexually transmitted infections, such as chlamydia and/or herpes simplex virus 2, and having an uncircumcised male partner (ACS, 2006a; Anttila, et al., 2001; CDC, 1999; Moscicki, 2005; NCI, 1999b).

Certain high risk HPV types are also now considered to be a cause of many cancers of the vagina, vulva, anus, and penis. Although each of these cancers occurs less frequently than cervical cancer, taken together they equal more than the number of cases of cervical cancer in the U.S. (ACS, 2006b). The average age for diagnosis of these cancers is significantly later than for cervical cancer. The median age of diagnosis for vaginal cancer is 68 years and 69 years for vulvar cancer. Anal cancer is typically diagnosed at 63 years of age for women and 58 years for men, and the average age of diagnosis for cancer of the penis is 68 years (Ries, et al., 2006). As is the case with cervical cancer, HPV 16 and HPV 18 are most often associated with vaginal, vulvar, anal, and penile cancer (Eng & Butler, 1997). HPV is also associated with 20 percent of oropharyngeal (primarily the tongue and tonsils) cancers and 90 percent of skin cancers in immunocompromised patients (González, et al., 2002). An association has also been made between HPV and other oral, head, and neck cancers, although further research needs to be conducted to establish a causal relationship (Morek, et al., 2001; Schwartz, et al., 1998). Men are three times more likely than women to develop head and neck cancers (*HPV Treatment and Prevention Resource,* 2001).

Cited References

ACOG—American College of Obstetricians and Gynecologists. (2000, accessed 2001, May 23). "Make Decisions about Human Papillomavirus Based on Sound Medicine, Rather than Poltics." [Online.] http://www.acog.org/from_home/departments/dept_notice.cfm?recno=11&bulletin=1083.

ACS—American Cancer Society. (2006a, February 9, accessed 2006, May 17). *Cervical Cancer,* Atlanta, GA: American Cancer Society Inc. [Online]. http://documents.cancer.org/115.00/115.00.pdf.

————.(2006b). *Cancer Facts and Figures 2006.* Atlanta, GA: American Cancer Society, Inc.

Anttila, Tarja, et al. (2001). "Serotypes of Chlamydia trachomatis and Risk for Development of Cervical Squamous Cell Carcinoma." *The Journal of the American Medical Association,* 285(1), 47–51.

Bosch, F. Xavier, and Silvia de Sanjosé. (2003). "Chapter 1: Human Papillomavirus and Cervical Cancer—Burden and Assessment of Causality." *Journal of the National Cancer Institute Monograph,* 31, 3–13.

CDC—Centers for Disease Control and Prevention. (1999, accessed 1999, October 1). *STD Trends.* [Online]. http://www.cdc.gov/nchstp/dstd/Stats_Trends/STD_Trends/pdf.

"The Cervical Cancer Virus." (1995). *Discover,* 16, 24–6.

Clifford, G.M., et al. (2003). "Human Papillomavirus Types in Invasive Cervical Cancer Worldwide: A Meta-Analysis." *British Journal of Cancer*, 88(1), 63–73.

Eng, Thomas, and William Butler, eds. (1997). *The Hidden Epidemic: Confronting Sexually Transmitted Diseases*. Washington, DC: National Academy Press.

González Intxaurraga, M.A., et al. (2002). "HPV and Carcinogenesis." *Acta Dermatolvenerol*, 11(3), 1–8.

Ho, Gloria Y.F., et al. (1995). "Persistent Genital Human Papillomavirus Infection as a Risk Factor for Persistent Cervical Dysplasia." *Journal of the National Cancer Institute*, 87(18), 1365–71.

HPV Treatment and Prevention Resource: New Opportunities, New Challenges. (2001). Decatur, GA: Flynn Publications.

Janicek, Mike, and Hervy Averette. (2001). "Cervical Cancer: Prevention, Diagnosis, and Therapeutics." *CA: A Cancer Journal for Clinicians*, 51(2), 92–114.

Kay, Jane. (2005, February 1, accessed 2006, May 19). "X-Rays Added To Cancer List; Some Viruses Also Among Carcinogens on Federal Registry." *San Francisco Chronicle*, p. A1.

Morek, Jon, et al. (2001). "Human Papillomavirus Infection as a Risk Factor for Squamous-Cell Carcinoma of the Head and Neck." *New England Journal of Medicine*, 344(15), 1125–31.

Moscicki, Anna-Barbara. (2005). "Impact of HPV Infection in Adolescent Populations." *Journal of Adolescent Health*, 37, S3–9.

Muñoz, Nubia, et al. (2003). "Epidemiologic Classification of Human Papillomavirus Types Associated with Cervical Cancer." New England Journal of Medicine, 348(6), 518–27.

NCI—National Cancer Institute. (1999a, accessed 2001, May 21). *Cervical Cancer: Backgrounder.* [Online]. http://rex.nci.nih.gov/massmedia/backgrounders/cervical. html.

Ries, L.A.G., et al., eds. (2005, posted 2006, accessed 2006, May 19). *SEER Cancer Statistics Review,* 1975-2003. Bethesda, MD: National Cancer Institute. [Online]. http://seer.cancer.gov/csr/19752003/.

Schiffman, Mark, and Philip E. Castle. (2003). "Human Papillomavirus: Epidemiology and Public Health." *Archives of Pathology and Laboratory Medicine,* 127, 930–4.

Schwartz, Stephen, et al. (1998, November 4). "Oral Cancer Risk in Relation to Sexual History and Evidence of Human Papillomavirus Infection." *Journal of the National Cancer Institute,* 90(21), 1626–36.

Shah, Keerti V. (1997). "Human Papillomaviruses and Anogential Cancers." *The New England Journal of Medicine,* 337(19), 1386–8.

Walboomers, J.M., et al. (1999). "Human Papillomavirus Is a Necessary Cause of Invasive Cervical Cancer Worldwide." *Journal of Pathology,* 189(1), 12–9.

WHO—World Health Organization, Initiative for Vaccine Research. (2005, January). *State of the Art of Vaccine Research and Development.* Geneva, Switzerland: World Health Organization. [Online]. http://www.who.int/vaccine_research/documents/Dip%20814.pdf.

———. (2006). *Comprehensive Cervical Cancer Control: A Guide to Essential Practice.* Geneva, Switzerland: World Health Organization. [Online]. http://www.who.int/reproductive-health/publications/cervical_cancer_gep/text.pdf.

Wiley, D.J., et al. (2002). "External Genital Warts: Diagnosis, Treatment, and Prevention." *Clinical Infectious Diseases,* 35(Suppl 2), S210-24.

Chemotherapy Is an Effective Cancer Treatment

HisandHerHealth.com

HisandHerHealth.com is a cutting-edge Web site that provides information on the latest sex-related medical news for men and women.

Chemotherapy has been shown to greatly increase the cure of certain types of cancers. New research and development is constantly evolving the way cancer is treated, but chemotherapy continues to be a promising treatment for many patients.

The race to cure cancer has been a marathon physicians and researchers have been running for decades. But, since the advent of chemotherapeutic treatments, more hurdles are being cleared than ever before. For without surgery and effective, though toxic, drugs to stop cancers in their tracks, many cancer victims might not be the survivors they are today. . . .

Chemotherapy Increases Cure Rates in Some Cancers

Thanks to chemotherapy, some urologic cancers—such as testicular, bladder and Wilms tumor—have a much higher rate of cure. The most striking chemotherapeutic advances—drugs such as cisplatin, bleomycin and etoposide—have made testicular cancer, the most common malignancy in young men, also the most treatable. Three decades ago, if these "germ cell tumors" had metastasized, the patient usually died. But, today's anti-cancer drugs can produce cures even of the far advanced testicular cancer, remissions for prostate cancer and prolonged remissions and cures for bladder cancer patients.

HisandHerHealth.com, "Chemotherapy: Knocking Out Cancer with Chemotherapy," medically reviewed by John P. Donahue, M.D. and George F. Bosl, M.D., 2006. www .hisandherhealth.com. © 2006 Vibrance Associates, LLC. All rights reserved. Reproduced by permission.

In 1910, German bacteriologist Paul Ehrlich gave momentum to selectively targeting toxic chemicals for specific diseases by using salvarsan to treat syphilis. Paving the way for antibacterial drugs, Ehrlich's work also piqued the interest in similar "magic bullets" for cancer.

While University of Chicago's Charles B. Huggins (a Nobel laureate), C.V. Hodges and W.W. Scott introduced hormone therapy for advanced prostate cancer in 1941, headway on testicular cancer treatment was not made until the 1960s, when actinomycin D became a standard. Some 40 percent to 50 percent of patients responded while 10 percent achieved complete remission.

By the mid-1970s, University of Texas M.D. Anderson [Cancer Center]'s Melvin L. Samuels capitalized on the synergistic benefits of vinblastine and bleomycin. By combining drugs that interrupted different stages of the cell cycle, Samuels increased the proportion of patients who experienced response and remission.

Drug Breakthroughs Have Increased Survival Chances

An important breakthrough came in 1965 when Barnett Rosenberg, a Michigan State University chemist, discovered that platinum analogues inhibited bacterial growth. Out of this research grew cisplatin, a compound that would prove to have anti-tumor effects. Today, cisplatin is an essential ingredient in many of today's chemotherapeutic regimens, including testicular and bladder cancer. It places itself between DNA strands in such a way that rapidly dividing abnormal cells cannot replicate, producing cell death and tumor shrinkage. If shrinkage is great enough, then complete tumor disappearance is possible.

Clinical trials of cisplatin began in the early 1970s, led by Roswell Park [Cancer Institute]'s D.J. Higby and H.J. Wallace, who observed responses in testicular cancer. Memorial Sloan-

Kettering [Cancer Center]'s Robert B. Golbey and Indiana University's Lawrence H. Einhorn confirmed the drug's potency against testicular cancer. The biggest breakthrough came when Einhorn and John P. Donohue reported in 1977 that the combination of cisplatin, vinblastine and bleomycin together with surgery after chemotherapy could achieve complete remissions in up to 85 percent of patients. For patients with a durable complete remission, doctors could eventually "cure" 70 to 80 percent of testicular cancer patients. Urologists had more varied success with other cancers. Memorial Sloan Kettering Cancer Center's Alan Yagoda led the research in the 1970s and 1980s to develop a combination—methotrexate vinblastine, Adriamycin and cisplatin (MVAC)—that would result in two-thirds of bladder cancer patients achieving remission. Other scientists confirmed that MVAC could shrink bladder cancer, permitting surgical or radiological interventions. This treatment plan generally produced short-term results, since only 10 percent of bladder cancer patients were disease-free after five years.

Scientists are searching for effective agents that improve survival, while producing fewer side effects.

During the 1980–90s, less-toxic but equally effective drugs were studied. For testicular cancer, etoposide replaced vinblastine. Based on work at Indiana University and Memorial Sloan-Kettering, the regimen prescribed most often for testicular cancer today is etoposide and cisplatin with or without bleomycin. For bladder cancer, gemcitabine + cisplatin was shown to be as effective as MVAC. Androgen-blocking Casodex and flutamide are now keystones in treating metastatic prostate cancer, and chemotherapeutic combinations are showing early promise in hormone-resistant disease. In children, drugs have boosted the cure rate of pediatric Wilm's tumor to 80 percent. Unfortunately, progress is limited for recurrent kidney cancer; interleukin-2 and alpha interferon rarely produce complete remissions, and standard cytotoxic [cell-killing] chemotherapy does not work.

The Search for Improvement Continues

As with other urologic cancers, scientists are searching for effective agents that improve survival, while producing fewer side effects. With no magic bullets expected, they are focused on finding targeted agents that can manipulate the molecular pathways that result in cancer. Advances in drug therapy will always be incorporated into progress with surgery and radiation therapy in order to give best results. Meticulous clinical trials are the only way to improve today's standard of care.

Whatever endurance it takes to finish this research race, the win will be worth the effort.

Chemotherapy Is Not an Effective Cancer Treatment

Dani Veracity

Dani Veracity is a health writer for NewsTarget.com, an online news site.

Generally accepted as the norm for treatment in cancer, chemotherapy is just as toxic to the patient as it is to the cancer cells. The side effects of chemotherapy are extreme—weight loss, hair loss, vomiting—and indicate the trauma going on inside the patient's body, as both good and bad cells are attacked by this treatment. In most cases patients, in consultation with a medical professional, should consider all possible treatments before resorting to chemotherapy.

> If cancer specialists were to admit publicly that chemotherapy is of limited usefulness and is often dangerous, the public might demand a radical change in direction—possibly toward unorthodox and nontoxic methods, and toward cancer prevention.... The use of chemotherapy is even advocated by those members of the establishment who realize how ineffective and dangerous it can be. —Ralph W. Moss, author, *The Cancer Industry*

Imagine that you own a house that is absolutely perfect and beautiful, with all the necessities, except that it has some rodents inside. When you call the exterminators, they tell you that they won't be able to target just the rodents, as these rodents are of an especially stealthy breed. They tell you they're just going to set off a series of explosions in your house that may kill the rodents. They warn you, "Oh yeah, it may destroy some of your house in the process, but, hey, you want those rodents out of your house, right?" There's probably no way you would allow that; instead, you would do some research and find other, more specific and less generally destructive ways of getting rid of the rodents.

The allegorical exterminators' logic makes no sense; yet, it's the same logic that doctors who prescribe chemotherapy follow. Like the exterminators' explosions, chemotherapy doesn't exclusively target cancer cells; it also harms your good cells, destroying some of your body—your "house"—in the process. As a result, many chemotherapy patients lose their hair, develop immune deficiencies, lose weight and vomit. Chemotherapy poisons your body as a whole in an attempt to kill the cancer cells before the "treatment" brings your body to an unrecoverable state.

As Gary Null and James Feast write, "(After chemotherapy,) the hope is the cancer is going to be totally dead and you are only half dead and [will] recover." Unfortunately, some people are more than "half dead" after chemotherapy and remain damaged for the rest of their lives, no matter how long or how short that life may be. They never realize that according to many alternative health practitioners, there are safer ways of combating many types of cancer.

Side Effects of Chemo Are Tremendous

Former chemotherapy patient Anne explains in Michio Kushi's and Alex Jack's book, *The Cancer Prevention Diet*: "My mind rebelled at the thought of another six months of that poison. On several occasions, the doctor couldn't perform chemotherapy treatments on me because my white blood cell count was dangerously low. I promised my body I would not undergo any further chemotherapy treatments."

Anne's account reflects the feelings of all too many cancer patients who have suffered through months of often debilitating chemotherapy. The side effects that chemotherapy patients feel and others see—the extreme nausea and vomiting, the hair loss, the weight loss—are indicative of the intense havoc that chemotherapy is causing within the body. According to the Life Extension Foundation, chemotherapy drugs are "cytotoxic," meaning that "they kill cells that are extremely active." Cancer cells are, of course, extremely active. However, so are the cells of the hair and the immune system, for example, which accounts for chemotherapy's destructive side effects.

As if these side effects are not enough, cancer therapy commonly includes surgery and radiation, both of which have their own dangers and side effects. As Professor Null writes in his *Complete Encyclopedia of Natural Healing*, "The mainstream medical establishment often prescribes mastectomy, radiation and chemotherapy to treat cancer, an approach that has been described as a slash-and-burn strategy." The treatment for breast cancer is unfortunately often the general rule among cancer treatments—cut off the affected organ, poison the body with chemotherapy and then harm the body even more with radiation.

The most extreme example of unnecessary cancer therapy—treatment for false positive cancer diagnoses—is more common then we'd like to believe.

In *Get Healthy Now*, Professor Null describes one woman's experience with mainstream medicine's approach to breast cancer treatment: "Three days later, she had her breast lopped off. That was followed up with lots of chemotherapy. Her hair fell out and she vomited 24 hours a day. She couldn't keep any food down. Then they did radiation and her skin burnt up and two of her ribs broke." He concludes, "Most people don't know how dangerous radiation is. I had seen enough. I wouldn't touch any of that medicine with a 10-foot pole." Surgical removal of the cancerous body part also has its own aftereffects, of course, requiring not only the normal recovery after any surgery, but also coping with the psychological effects of having a body part removed.

Unnecessary in the First Place

As cancer patients suffer from the side effects of chemotherapy and other methods of mainstream cancer treatment, the fact remains that according to many medical practitioners, these treatments are unnecessary and sometimes do more harm than good. In response to chemotherapy's many side effects, Dr. [Robert] Atkins says in Burton Goldberg's *Alternative Medicine*, "Only in situations in which chemotherapy is proven to be effective and curative would I recommend it. In general, this might be testicular cancer."

Many people also think that surgery can sometimes do more harm than good: Biopsy, for example, may in fact spread cancer cells, according to Professor Null. Furthermore, the most extreme example of unnecessary cancer therapy—treatment for false positive cancer diagnoses—is more common than we'd like to believe, according to *Critical Condition* authors Donald L. Barlett and James B. Steele.

There Are Alternatives

If, as many people believe, mainstream cancer treatment is sometimes ineffective and always harmful to the body as a whole, then what is the alternative? Goldberg writes that Ukrain, which is made from the alkaloids of the greater celandine plant and the pharmaceutical Thiotepa, "can do everything chemotherapy does but without the side effects, so it renders chemotherapy largely unnecessary." The beauty of Ukrain is that, unlike chemotherapy drugs, it only targets the cancer cells and not your healthy ones. Furthermore, good nutrition—vitamins, minerals, fiber, fresh fruit and vegetables, juices and medicinal herbs—can do wonders against cancer. Of course, you need to discuss a treatment plan that is right for your type of cancer and your body with a medical professional, preferably a naturopath. But, before you say yes to chemotherapy, remember what it does to your body and consider all available treatments.

Gene Therapy Is a Promising Cancer Treatment

National Cancer Institute

The National Cancer Institute is a federal institution providing cancer information to the public.

Gene therapy is an experimental treatment that involves introducing genetic material into a person's cells to fight disease. Although current methods of introducing genetic material are often risky, researchers are actively developing new methods of delivery to increase the success rate of this treatment. In addition to risk factors, gene therapy is sometimes viewed as being ethically and socially questionable because some see the altering of the genetic makeup of humans as dangerous. To date, however, gene therapy remains a promising treatment for cancer.

Genes are the biological units of heredity. Genes determine obvious traits, such as hair and eye color, as well as more subtle characteristics, such as the ability of the blood to carry oxygen. Complex characteristics, such as physical strength, may be shaped by the interaction of a number of different genes along with environmental influences.

A gene is part of a deoxyribonucleic acid (DNA) molecule. Humans have between 50,000 and 100,000 genes. Genes carry instructions that allow the cells to produce specific proteins such as enzymes. During the creation of proteins, cells use another molecule, ribonucleic acid (RNA), to translate the genetic information stored in DNA. Only certain genes in a cell are active at any given moment. As cells mature, many genes become permanently inactive. The pattern of active and inac-

National Cancer Institute, "Gene Therapy for Cancer: Questions and Answers," National Cancer Institute Fact Sheet, March 3, 2004. www.cancer.gov/cancertopics/factsheet/Therapy/gene.

tive genes in a cell and the resulting protein composition determine what kind of cell it is and what it can and cannot do. Flaws in genes can result in disease.

Gene therapy . . . involves introducing genetic material (DNA or RNA) into a person's cells to fight disease.

Gene Therapy

Advances in understanding and manipulating genes have set the stage for scientists to alter patients' genetic material to fight or prevent disease. Gene therapy is an experimental treatment that involves introducing genetic material (DNA or RNA) into a person's cells to fight disease. Gene therapy is being studied in clinical trials (research studies with humans) for many different types of cancer and for other diseases. It is not currently available outside a clinical trial.

Gene Therapy in Cancer Treatment

Researchers are studying several ways to treat cancer using gene therapy. Some approaches target healthy cells to enhance their ability to fight cancer. Other approaches target cancer cells, to destroy them or prevent their growth. Some gene therapy techniques under study are described below.

- In one approach, researchers replace missing or altered genes with healthy genes. Because some missing or altered genes (e.g., p53) may lead to cancer, substituting "working" copies of these genes may keep cancer from developing.

- Researchers are also studying ways to improve a patient's immune response to cancer. In this approach, gene therapy is used to stimulate the body's natural ability to attack cancer cells.

- In some studies, scientists inject cancer cells with genes that make them more sensitive to chemotherapy, radiation therapy, or other treatments. In other studies, researchers place a gene into healthy blood-forming stem cells to make these cells more resistant to the side effects of high doses of anticancer drugs.

- In another approach, researchers inject cancer cells with genes that can be used to destroy the cells. In this technique, "suicide genes" are introduced into cancer cells. Later, a pro-drug (an inactive form of a toxic drug) is given to the patient. The pro-drug is activated in cancer cells containing these "suicide genes," which leads to the destruction of those cancer cells.

- Other research is focused on the use of gene therapy to prevent cancer cells from developing new blood vessels (angiogenesis).

How Gene Transfer Takes Place

In general, a gene cannot be directly inserted into a person's cell. It must be delivered to the cell using a carrier, or "vector." The vectors most commonly used in gene therapy are viruses. Viruses have a unique ability to recognize certain cells and insert their DNA into the cells.

In some gene therapy clinical trials, cells from the patient's blood or bone marrow are removed and grown in the laboratory. The cells are exposed to the virus that is carrying the desired gene. The virus enters the cells and inserts the desired gene into the cells' DNA. The cells grow in the laboratory and are then returned to the patient by injection into a vein. This type of gene therapy is called *ex vivo* because the cells are grown outside the body. The gene is transferred into the patient's cells while the cells are outside the patient's body.

In other studies, vectors (often viruses) or liposomes (fatty particles) are used to deliver the desired gene to cells in the patient's body. This form of gene therapy is called *in vivo*, because the gene is transferred to cells inside the patient's body.

Types of Viruses Used in Gene Therapy

Many gene therapy clinical trials rely on retroviruses to deliver the desired gene. Other viruses used as vectors include adenoviruses, adeno-associated viruses, lentiviruses, poxviruses, and herpes viruses. These viruses differ in how well they transfer the genes to cells, which cells they can recognize and infect, and whether they alter the cell's DNA permanently or temporarily. Thus, researchers may use different vectors, depending on the specific characteristics and requirements of the study.

Scientists alter the viruses used in gene therapy to make them safe for humans and to increase their ability to deliver specific genes to a patient's cells. Depending on the type of virus and the goals of the research study, scientists may inactivate certain genes in the viruses to prevent them from reproducing or causing disease. Researchers may also alter the virus so that it better recognizes and enters the target cell.

Scientists need to identify more efficient ways to deliver genes to the body.

The Risks

Viruses can usually infect more than one type of cell. Thus, when viral vectors are used to carry genes into the body, they might infect healthy cells as well as cancer cells. Another danger is that the new gene might be inserted in the wrong location in the DNA, possibly causing cancer or other harmful mutations to the DNA.

In addition, when viruses or liposomes are used to deliver DNA to cells inside the patient's body, there is a slight chance that this DNA could unintentionally be introduced into the patient's reproductive cells. If this happens, it could produce changes that may be passed on if a patient has children after treatment.

Other concerns include the possibility that transferred genes could be "overexpressed," producing so much of the missing protein as to be harmful; that the viral vector could cause inflammation or an immune reaction; and that the virus could be transmitted from the patient to other individuals or into the environment.

Scientists use animal testing and other precautions to identify and avoid these risks before any clinical trials are conducted in humans.

Some Problems with Gene Therapy

Scientists need to identify more efficient ways to deliver genes to the body. To treat cancer and other diseases effectively with gene therapy, researchers must develop vectors that can be injected into the patient and specifically focus on the target cells located throughout the body. More work is also needed to ensure that the vectors will successfully insert the desired genes into each of these target cells.

Researchers also need to be able to deliver genes consistently to a precise location in the patient's DNA, and ensure that transplanted genes are precisely controlled by the body's normal physiologic signals.

Although scientists are working hard on these problems, it is impossible to predict when they will have effective solutions.

Gene therapy is currently focused on correcting genetic flaws and curing life-threatening disease.

Social and Ethical Issues

In large measure, the [social and ethical] issues are the same as those faced whenever a powerful new technology is developed. Such technologies can accomplish great good, but they can also result in great harm if applied unwisely.

Gene therapy is currently focused on correcting genetic flaws and curing life-threatening disease, and regulations are in place for conducting these types of studies. But in the future, when the techniques of gene therapy have become simpler and more accessible, society will need to deal with more complex questions.

One such question is related to the possibility of genetically altering human eggs or sperm, the reproductive cells that pass genes on to future generations. (Because reproductive cells are also called germ cells, this type of gene therapy is referred to as germ-line therapy.) Another question is related to the potential for enhancing human capabilities—for example, improving memory and intelligence—by genetic intervention. Although both germ-line gene therapy and genetic enhancement have the potential to produce benefits, possible [social and ethical] problems with these procedures worry many scientists.

Germ-line gene therapy would forever change the genetic make-up of an individual's descendants. Thus, the human gene pool would be permanently affected. Although these changes would presumably be for the better, an error in technology or judgment could have far-reaching consequences. The NIH [National Institutes of Health] does not approve germ-line gene therapy in humans.

In the case of genetic enhancement, there is concern that such manipulation could become a luxury available only to the rich and powerful. Some also fear that widespread use of this technology could lead to new definitions of "normal" that would exclude individuals who are, for example, of merely average intelligence. And, justly or not, some people associate all genetic manipulation with past abuses of the concept of "eugenics," or the study of methods of improving genetic qualities through selective breeding.

Hormone Therapy May Be Effective as a Cancer Treatment

Mayo Clinic

The Mayo Clinic specializes in the latest medical treatments available and provides information on current medical issues.

Rarely used alone, hormone therapy is often used to treat hormone-sensitive cancers such as prostate cancer. In addition to treating existing cancer, scientists are exploring the possibility that hormone therapy could prevent cancer in people with a family history or who are at a high risk for developing certain types of cancer. Like any treatment, there are side effects to hormone therapy, and any decisions should be made with a physician, but hormone therapy can be part of a successful treatment plan.

The term "hormone therapy" might make you think of women taking estrogen to reduce their symptoms of menopause or men taking testosterone to slow the effects of aging. But hormone therapy for cancer—also called endocrine therapy—is something completely different. Hormone therapy for cancer alters the hormones in your body to help control or cure cancer.

Hormone therapies associated with menopause and aging seek to increase the amount of certain hormones in your body to compensate for age- or disease-related hormonal declines. But hormone therapy as a cancer treatment either reduces the level of specific hormones in your body or alters your cancer's ability to use these hormones to grow and spread.

If your cancer is one that is sensitive to hormones, you might benefit from hormone therapy as part of your cancer treatment. Learn the basics of hormone therapy, how it works as a cancer treatment and its side effects. That way you'll be prepared to discuss it if your doctor recommends it as a cancer treatment option.

How Hormone Therapy Cancer Treatment Works

Specific types of tumors—most commonly tumors of the breast and of the prostate—rely on hormones such as estrogen and testosterone to survive and grow. Hormone therapy is a cancer treatment that attacks these hormone-dependent tumors in two ways:

- *Reducing hormones in your body.* By reducing the level of estrogen or testosterone in your body, hormone therapy cuts off the supply of hormones your cancer relies on for its survival.

- *Changing your cancer's ability to use hormones.* Synthetic hormones can bind to your cancer's hormone receptors, blocking your cancer's ability to get the hormones it needs for growth.

By altering your cancer's hormone supply, hormone therapy can make your tumors shrink. But this cancer treatment only works for hormone-sensitive cancers.

If your cancer is hormone-sensitive, you might benefit from hormone therapy.

People with Hormone-Sensitive Cancers Benefit

If your cancer is hormone-sensitive, you might benefit from hormone therapy as part of your cancer treatment. Your doctor can tell you whether or not your cancer is sensitive to hormones. This is usually determined by taking a sample of your tumor (biopsy) for analysis in a laboratory.

Cancers that are most likely to be hormone-receptive include:

- Breast cancer

- Prostate cancer

- Ovarian cancer

- Endometrial cancer

Not every cancer of these types is hormone-sensitive, however. That's why the cells of your cancer must be analyzed to determine if hormone therapy is appropriate for you.

Uses for Hormone Therapy
Cancer Treatment

Hormone therapy is rarely used as a main (primary) cancer treatment. It's usually used in combination with other types of cancer treatments, including surgery, radiation and chemotherapy.

Your doctor might use a hormone therapy before you begin a primary cancer treatment, such as before surgery to remove a tumor. This is called neoadjuvant therapy. Hormone therapy can sometimes shrink a tumor to a more manageable size so that it's easier to remove during surgery.

Researchers are also exploring the use of hormone therapies to prevent cancer from occurring in people with a high risk of cancer.

Hormone therapy is sometimes given in addition to the primary treatment—usually after—in an effort to prevent the cancer from recurring (adjuvant therapy). If you've had surgery to remove your tumor and it appears that all of your cancer has been removed, your doctor might use hormone therapy to try to keep your cancer from coming back.

In some cases of advanced (metastatic) cancers, such as in advanced prostate cancer and advanced breast cancer, hormone therapy is sometimes used as the main treatment.

Researchers are also exploring the use of hormone therapies to prevent cancer from occurring in people with a high risk of cancer.

Forms of Hormone Therapy

Hormone therapy can be given in several forms, including:

Surgery Surgery can reduce the levels of hormones in your body by removing the parts of your body that produce the hormones, including:

- Testicles (orchiectomy, or castration)

- Ovaries (oophorectomy) in premenopausal women

- Adrenal gland (adrenalectomy) in postmenopausal women

- Pituitary gland (hypophysectomy) in women

Because certain drugs can duplicate the hormone-suppressive effects of surgery in many situations, drugs are used more often than surgery for hormone therapy. And because removal of the testicles or ovaries will limit an individual's options when it comes to having children, younger people are more likely to choose drugs over surgery.

Radiation Radiation is used to suppress the production of hormones. Just as is true of surgery, it's used most commonly to stop hormone production in the testicles, ovaries, and adrenal and pituitary glands. Your doctor might recommend radiation therapy rather than surgery if surgery is too risky for you or if it carries too many side effects.

Drugs Various drugs can alter your body's production of estrogen and testosterone. These can be taken in pill form or by means of injection. The most common types of drugs for hormone-receptive cancers include:

Anti-hormones Anti-hormones block your cancer cells' ability to interact with the hormones that propel your cancer's growth. Though these drugs don't reduce your body's production of hormones, anti-hormones block your cancer's ability to use these hormones. Anti-hormones include the anti-estrogens tamoxifen (Nolvadex) and toremifene (Fareston) for breast cancer, and the anti-androgens flutamide (Eulexin) and bicalutamide (Casodex) for prostate cancer.

Aromatase inhibitors Aromatase inhibitors (AIs) target enzymes that produce estrogen in postmenopausal women, thus reducing the amount of estrogen available to fuel tumors. AIs are only used in postmenopausal women because the drugs can't prevent the production of estrogen in women who haven't yet been through menopause. Approved AIs include letrozole (Femara), anastrozole (Arimidex) and exemestane (Aromasin). It has yet to be determined if AIs are helpful for men with cancer.

Most side effects of hormone therapy are temporary.

Luteinizing hormone-releasing hormone (LH-RH) agonists and antagonists LH-RH agonists—sometimes called analogs— and LH-RH antagonists reduce the level of hormones in your body by altering the mechanisms in your brain that tell your body to produce hormones.

LH-RH agonists are essentially a chemical alternative to surgery for removal of the ovaries for women, or of the testicles for men. Depending on your cancer type, you might choose this route if you hope to have children in the future and want to avoid surgical castration. In most cases the effects of these drugs are reversible.

Examples of LH-RH agonists include:

- Leuprolide (Lupron, Viadur, Eligard) for prostate cancer

- Goserelin (Zoladex) for breast and prostate cancers

- Triptorelin (Trelstar) for ovarian and prostate cancers

One LH-RH antagonist is currently approved for men with prostate cancer—abarelix (Plenaxis)—and is also under investigation for use in women with breast cancer.

Side Effects of Hormone Therapy

Most of the side effects of hormone therapy are temporary. However, surgery and radiation can cause permanent damage to your ovaries or testicles.

Common side effects in men undergoing hormone therapy include:

- Decrease in sexual desire

- Enlarged breasts

- Hot flashes

- Inability to achieve an erection

- Incontinence

- Osteoporosis

In women undergoing hormone therapy, side effects can include symptoms similar to those of menopause, such as:

- Fatigue

- Hot flashes

- Mood swings

- Nausea

- Osteoporosis

- Weight gain

Effects of Hormone Therapy May Be Limited

If you opt for hormone therapy as a cancer treatment, be aware that the effects of hormone therapy may be limited. Most advanced hormone-sensitive cancers eventually become resistant to hormone treatment and find ways to thrive without hormones.

For instance, many women who've had surgery for breast cancer take tamoxifen only for five years because taking it for a longer period doesn't offer any further benefit and may actually increase the risk that cancer will recur. But you're not out of options at the end of those five years. Your doctor may prescribe another form of hormone therapy to which your cancer may respond. Women who've taken tamoxifen may be able to take an aromatase inhibitor, such as letrozole.

If you have prostate cancer, your doctor might prescribe intermittent dosing of hormone therapy drugs in an attempt to prevent your cancer from becoming resistant to therapy. This means you won't take a drug continuously for several years. Instead you'll start and stop taking the drug as your doctor closely monitors your cancer.

Other Hormone Treatments for Cancer

Certain cancers produce excessive levels of hormones. Though rare, cancers such as carcinoid tumors, pheochromocytomas and other neuroendocrine cancers lead to production of these higher levels of your body's natural hormones. The excess hormones can cause such signs and symptoms as sweating, flushing, high blood pressure and diarrhea. Your doctor might prescribe hormone-blocking drugs to reduce these symptoms.

Immunotherapy and Vaccines Are the Ultimate Cancer Treatment

Michelle Meadows

Michelle Meadows writes for the FDA Consumer, *a publication of the U.S. Food and Drug Adminstration.*

While radiation and chemotherapy are sometimes effective, these treatments are damaging to the body and clearly have limitations. Cancer vaccines are the new cutting-edge treatment that train the immune system to attack cancer cells. Although cancer vaccines are still being tested, and are not yet FDA approved, early studies show promise that cancer vaccines can be a viable treatment for certain types of cancer.

Vaccines traditionally have been used to prevent infectious diseases such as measles and the flu. But with cancer vaccines, the emphasis is on treatment, at least for now. The idea is to inject a preparation of inactivated cancer cells or proteins that are unique to cancer cells into a person who has cancer. The goal: to train the person's immune system to recognize the living cancer cells and attack them.

Cancer Vaccines Are Experimental

"The best settings are for treating people who have minimal disease or a high risk of recurrence," says Jeffrey Schlom, Ph.D., chief of the Laboratory of Tumor Immunology and Biology at the National Cancer Institute (NCI). "But at this time, most therapeutic cancer vaccines are being studied in people who have failed other therapies."

Michelle Meadows, "Cancer Vaccines: Training the Immune System to Fight Cancer," *FDA Consumer*, vol. 38, December 2004, pp. 20–25. Reproduced by permission.

Cancer vaccines are experimental; none have been licensed by the Food and Drug Administration [FDA]. But there are about a dozen cancer vaccines in advanced clinical trials, says Steven Hirschfeld, M.D., a medical officer in the FDA's Center for Biologics Evaluation and Research. "Research has shown us that the fundamental approach to cancer vaccines is right; we are moving in the right direction," he says.

The three standard cancer therapies are surgery to remove tumors; chemotherapy, which modifies or destroys cancer cells with drugs; and radiation, which destroys cancer cells with high-energy X-rays. Immunotherapy, which includes cancer vaccines, is considered a fourth, and still investigational, type of therapy. Cancer vaccines are sometimes used alone, but are often combined with a standard therapy.

Cancer vaccines are designed to be specific, targeting only the cancer cells without harming the healthy ones.

Standard Cancer Treatments Are Limited

While standard treatments alone have proven effective, they also have limitations. Radiation and chemotherapy can wipe out a person's cancer cells, but they also damage normal cells. "We want to find treatment that is more targeted and less toxic," says Hirschfeld. "Cancer vaccines are designed to be specific, targeting only the cancer cells without harming the healthy ones."

The approach has made cancer vaccines generally well tolerated, allowing them to be used in outpatient settings. And they can be added to standard therapy with a low likelihood of causing further serious side effects.

How Cancer Vaccines Work

Cancer is a term for more than 100 diseases characterized by the uncontrolled, abnormal growth of cells. To the immune system—the body's natural defense system against disease—cancer cells and normal cells look the same. The immune system tends to tolerate the cancer cells, just as it tolerates the normal cells. That's because the immune system doesn't recognize cancer cells as something foreign, Hirschfeld says. Rather, cancer cells are once-normal cells that have gone awry. Cancer vaccines try to get the immune system to overcome its tolerance of cancer cells so that it can recognize them and attack them.

The two main approaches for cancer vaccines are whole-cell vaccines and antigen vaccines.

All cells have unique proteins or bits of proteins on their surface called antigens. Many cancer cells make cancer-specific antigens. The goal of using cancer antigens as a vaccine is to teach the immune system to recognize the cancer-specific antigens and to reject any cells with those antigens. The antigens activate white blood cells called B lymphocytes (B cells) and T lymphocytes (T cells). B cells produce antibodies that recognize a particular antigen and bind to it to help destroy the cancer cells. T cells that recognize a particular antigen can attack and kill cancer cells. In 1991, the first human cancer antigen was found in cells of a person with melanoma, a discovery that encouraged researchers to search for antigens on other types of cancer, according to the NCI.

The two main approaches for cancer vaccines are whole-cell vaccines and antigen vaccines. Whole-cell vaccines may take whole cancer cells from a patient or sometimes several patients, or use human tumor cell lines derived in a laboratory. "Some cell-based vaccines use tumor cells from the patient, some contain something that looks like a tumor cell but was created in a lab, and others are personalized vaccines that use some cells from the patient and some from the lab," Hirschfeld says. Cells that are taken from people with cancer are altered in a lab to inactivate them so that they are safe to re-inject.

Regardless of the exact source of the cells, whole-cell vaccines potentially use all the antigens found on the tumor cells. Antigen vaccines try to trigger an immune response by using only certain antigens from cancer cells. Hirschfeld says antigens may be particular to an individual, to a certain type of cancer, or to several types of cancers.

Boosting the Immune Response

In the early 1990s, Steven Rosenberg, M.D., one of the pioneers of immunotherapy and chief of surgery at the NCI, wrote that trying to use the immune system to fight cancer is so difficult that it made him feel "like a dog trying to bite a basketball." Among Rosenberg's contributions was identifying the antigens that trigger an immune response, and cloning genes that look for, or "code for," those antigens.

Researchers have been working to develop cancer vaccines for more than 100 years in one form or another, and the main mission has always been to make the immune system's response to the cancer antigens as strong as possible.

One major strategy involves combining vaccines with additional substances called adjuvants, which act as chemical messengers that help T cells work better. An example of one type of adjuvant, called a cytokine, is interleukin-2. This protein is made by the body's immune system and can also be made in a lab.

There have also been improvements in vaccine delivery. For example, Schlom developed a vaccine in which genes for tumor antigens are put into a weakened virus called a "vector" that delivers genetic materials to cells. This makes the tumor antigen more visible to the immune system. The CEA-TRICOM vaccine was developed at the NCI through a cooperative research and development agreement with Therion

Biologics in Cambridge, Mass. Researchers use the vaccinia virus, the same virus in the smallpox vaccine, as the vector. The carcinoembryonic antigen (CEA), which is found on most breast, lung, colon, and pancreatic tumors, is added to the virus. Researchers also add three molecules, called "costimulatory molecules," which serve as signals that make the vaccine more potent than it would be if the antigen were used alone. A similar vaccine developed under the NCI agreement with Therion is the PANVAC vaccine, which has now entered advanced study as a treatment for pancreatic cancer.

In addition to studying this type of virus-based technique, researchers at Duke University's Cancer Center in Durham, N.C., have been studying vaccines that mix white blood cells called dendritic cells with genetic material from a person's tumor.

Dendritic cells, which can activate T cells, work by looking around, finding antigens, and showing them to the fighter T cells. Researchers have found ways to increase the number of dendritic cells in a vaccine. "Employing millions of 'pumped up' dendritic cells can help elicit a strong immune response," says H. Kim Lyerly, M.D., director of the Duke cancer center.

Cancer vaccines have shown promise in clinical trials with many types of cancer.

Recent work by Lyerly and Duke investigators Michael Morse, M.D., and Timothy Clay, Ph.D., has focused on modifying dendritic cells with viruses so that they activate even stronger T cell responses against cancer antigens.

"This is an evolving area, and it's exciting to be able to make progress," says Lyerly. "For decades, people thought it wasn't even fundamentally possible to develop cancer vaccines, and here we are. The science behind cancer vaccines is leading us to believe that we will find the answers."

Cancer Vaccines Show Promise

As with any new treatment, cancer vaccines must be first studied in lab animals and then tested for safety and effectiveness in three phases of human studies, called "clinical trials," before they can be approved by the FDA. In Phase 1 clinical trials, cancer vaccines are used alone and studied for safety and to determine the proper dose. In Phase 2 trials, they are tested for effectiveness and may be used alone or in combination with another therapy. Phase 3 trials are large-scale studies testing effectiveness and usually comparing a vaccine with some standard therapy. Researchers are testing vaccines using various adjuvants, delivery methods, and types of antigens.

Cancer vaccines have shown promise in clinical trials with many types of cancer. According to Howard Streicher, M.D., a senior investigator with the NCI's Cancer Therapy Evaluation Program, it's too soon to say which cancers will be treated with vaccine therapy. The types of tumors that have proven most susceptible to vaccines so far, he says, are: skin cancer (melanoma); kidney cancer (renal cell); a group of cancers that affect the lymphatic system (lymphoma); a malignant tumor of the bone marrow (myeloma); and solid tumors, such as lung cancer. The most work has been done in the area of melanoma, a type of skin cancer in which treatment options are limited when the disease is in advanced stages.

"After having a tumor removed, about half of patients with stage III melanoma may have a recurrence, and we want to prevent that," Streicher says. "Chemotherapy doesn't work in this area, so our hope is that this could be just the right place for a vaccine."

James Mulé, M.D., Ph.D., associate director of the H. Lee Moffitt Cancer Center and Research Institute in Tampa, Fla., says, though some early studies have shown that some people's tumors shrank or even disappeared in response to a cancer vaccine, it's still early. Mulé was an investigator on the first study that tested dendritic cells in children. In the Phase 1 study, one 16-year-old with cancer that had spread to her lungs and spine showed significant shrinkage of tumors.

"There is promise in the sense that some of these vaccines can elicit a powerful immune response in some patients, but I think we have to be careful about getting too excited over early studies that can't be reproduced," Mulé says.

Vaccines Yet to Be FDA Approved

Jeffrey Weber, M.D., Ph.D., director of the Norris Melanoma Center at the University of Southern California, says there is also still a lot of work to be done in discovering new antigens and adjuvants and more sophisticated strategies to overcome the immune system's tolerance of cancer cells. "We are still discovering molecules that regulate the immune system, such as CTLA-4, so we're still in the dark in some areas," Weber says. Recent research has found that inhibiting CTLA-4 can help the immune system attack some tumors.

Experts say that no therapeutic cancer vaccine has been licensed yet because few Phase 3 studies have been completed, and those that have been completed did not meet their goals of demonstrating safety and effectiveness of the vaccine. "We are still working with industry to define the characteristics, including potency," says the FDA's Hirschfeld. "So a trial may look promising early on, but our job is to make sure it can be reproduced. We have to ask: 'Will this treatment work in the larger population?'"

One of the challenges is that cancer vaccines may produce different effects than those caused by cancer drugs. With cancer drugs, experts ask whether there is an objective, measurable response, such as tumor shrinkage. A cancer drug may cause tumors to shrink, but a person still may not live longer. With a cancer vaccine, there may be fewer signs of tumor shrinkage, but a person might live longer.

There aren't the same landmarks that you would see with traditional therapies, says Natalie Sacks, M.D., medical director in the clinical research division at San Francisco–based Cell Genesys, which is studying its vaccines, called GVAX, in people with prostate cancer, pancreatic cancer, leukemia, and myeloma. These whole-cell vaccines all use a hormone that stimulates immune response, called granulocyte macrophage colony stimulating factor (GM-CSF).

Cancer vaccines show the most promise at preventing a recurrence of cancer.

"As sponsors, we want to develop treatments and get them out to the market and help patients," Sacks says. "In the case of cytotoxic chemotherapies, the traditional endpoints used in drug development are shorter-term outcomes, such as tumor response and progression-free survival. Where I expect immunotherapy to be successful is in longer-term outcomes and increased survival. Because of the mechanism of action, the patient may not show an immediate response as is generally observed with standard chemotherapies, and the trial may take longer."

More Clinical Trials Are Needed

Cancer researchers say their work won't mean much if more people don't enroll in clinical trials. According to the NCI, less than 3 percent of U.S. adults with cancer participate in clinical trials.

If there is a standard treatment available for a type of cancer, the NCI recommends choosing it over an experimental therapy. Cancer vaccines show the most promise at preventing a recurrence of cancer after surgery, radiation, or chemotherapy because the immune system will need to recognize and attack a smaller number of cancer cells. Cancer vaccines are also being tested as a treatment for advanced cancer.

A Macrobiotic Diet Can Help Fight Cancer

Giselle Goodman

Giselle Goodman is a staff writer for the Portland Press Herald *in Maine.*

Meg Wolff is a cancer survivor who attributes her success to a macrobiotic diet. The diet includes organically grown vegetables, beans, and grains, and is endorsed by some doctors.

Collard greens for breakfast? Beans for dessert? Pickles with every meal?

These eats might not sound scrumptious to most folks, but for Meg Wolff of Cape Elizabeth, [Maine], they were a cure for cancer. She started eating nothing but grains, greens and beans in 1998 when she was diagnosed with aggressive breast cancer. Despite a mastectomy, chemotherapy and radiation, she continued to receive a glum forecast from her doctors. The cancer, doctors said, had spread to her lymph nodes and probably would be back in a year. It was a devastating blow to Wolff, who had lost her left leg to bone cancer seven years earlier.

Yet here she is six years later, cancer-free and feeling better than ever.

"Every day I just had a hard time getting out of bed, and nothing I did helped," she said. "I don't feel like I'd be here if it wasn't for the diet."

Macrobiotic Diets Are a Philosophy

The diet was a microbiotic one that is practiced all over the world by thousands of people who follow its philosophy that

Giselle Goodman, "Lifestyle for Healing," *Portland Press Herald*, March 4, 2004. Reproduced with permission of *Portland Press Herald/Maine Sunday Telegram*.

whole foods (grains, vegetables and beans), grown as organically and as locally as possible, are the keys to balance and harmony in body and mind.

Going on the diet was a tough transition for Wolff, who was a self-proclaimed junk-food junkie. As a child she craved fast food and snacks. She loved hamburgers and sweets. The macrobiotic diet required her to cast them off and adjust everything about her way of eating, even down to how often she chewed her food.

She had to shun animal fats, meats and dairy, although a piece of fish now and then is allowed. Processed foods and junk foods of any kind became no-nos. She traded in her sugar bowl for seaweed and her coffee for natural juices.

And the diet has to do with more than just eating. Those who follow it adhere to an entire philosophy that they are connected to the food they eat in a way that closes the gap between themselves and the natural world. They take nothing for granted—thought goes into every meal they make.

Many claim to have cured incurable diseases, like cancer, with the diet.

In Wolff's case, thought goes into every meal she does not eat.

"The toxins in the environment that cause cancer are stored in the fat of our bodies and animals," she said. "Basically, the more fat you take in, the more toxins you take in. Grains, beans and vegetables, especially the organics, have negative amounts of toxins compared to the animals."

Wolff is one of many people who have taken the diet to heart and swear by its consequences. Many claim to have cured incurable diseases, like cancer, with the diet.

Not All Doctors Are Against It

The diet isn't embraced by everybody, though. Some traditional doctors turn their backs on the philosophy, going so far as to warn against trying it because, they say, it causes too much weight loss during compromising treatments such as chemotherapy.

Dr. Dixie Mills, a breast surgeon who practices at Maine Medical Center and Women to Women in Portland, is not one of those doctors. She does not push her patients to try the diet, but when they seek advice about it she does not turn them away.

"I think there is a missing element in traditional breast cancer treatment," Mills said. "I think the idea of fruits and vegetables and multigrains is great. I think not using processed fats and not using processed white sugar is good, too."

In fact, she said, sometimes it seems like the better way to go.

"I cringe at the doughnuts that are served to cancer patients," she said. "They need it for comfort, but I think they could find something healthier."

For Wolff, healthy foods have become comfort food, so much so that her husband, son and daughter all eat the same macrobiotic diet.

A Change in Lifestyle

And she has become so committed to her diet that she has studied at the center where the philosophy of the macrobiotic diet was born—the Kushi Institute in Becket, Mass. She began attending macrobiotic diet conferences and established a Web site, www.macrobreastcancersurvivors.com, and she has been assisting in whole-foods cooking classes at the Cancer Community Center in South Portland.

She knows for many it's difficult to change a lifestyle of eating, but she said it is well worth it.

Her advice to beginners: add leafy green vegetables to any diet to make it healthier. Her favorites include kale, mustards, dandelion greens and watercress.

And, of course, the collard greens she eats for breakfast.

Vitamin E Does Not Prevent Cancer

Harvard Women's Health Watch

Harvard Women's Health Watch *is published by Harvard Medical School and covers a wide range of women's health topics.*

While vitamin E and aspirin can be good for you, they are not a miracle cure for cancer. Studies show that aspirin has no effect on the occurrence of cancer and findings related to the impact of vitamin E on the incidence of cancer have been inconsistent.

After one of the longest clinical trials ever completed, researchers conclude that regular use of aspirin and vitamin E does little or nothing to stave off heart disease or cancer.

These findings come from the Women's Health Study (WHS), the largest ever to study the effects of aspirin and vitamin E on disease prevention in women. The 10-year investigation involving nearly 40,000 subjects was led by researchers at Boston's Brigham and Women's Hospital. Earlier results from the same study showed that low-dose aspirin does not protect most women from a first heart attack, although it modestly reduces their risk of stroke. (Among women 65 and older, aspirin does reduce the risk of cardiovascular events, including heart attack and ischemic stroke.) Vitamin E supplements have long been touted for the prevention of chronic disease on the basis of animal studies and observational data, but there has been no adequate test until this study.

The findings, published in the July 6, 2005, *Journal of the American Medical Association*, leave open the possibility that higher doses of aspirin may be helpful. The WHS also established that it's safe to take vitamin E supplements at the level of 600 IU every other day, countering another analysis that suggested harm at 150 IU or higher per day, and particularly in excess of 400 IU per day.

Aspirin Is Not Effective Against Cancer

The Women's Health Study followed 39,876 healthy women ages 45 and older for an average of 10 years. Participants were randomly assigned to receive 100 milligrams of aspirin or a placebo every other day and 600 IU of vitamin E or a placebo on alternate days. Participants were monitored for cardiovascular events—heart attack, stroke, or death from cardiovascular causes—as well as overall cancer rates and cancer deaths.

Aspirin had no effect on the incidence of cancer or cancer deaths in general. It offered no protection against breast cancer or cancer at any other site except, possibly, the lung (further study is needed to explore this possibility). In a subsidiary analysis, vitamin E reduced cardiovascular deaths by 24% in general and cardiovascular disease risk by 26% in women ages 65 and over, who constituted 10% of the study participants. The investigators note that these findings are inconsistent with data from other studies and thus require further research.

Stick to Traditional Preventive Medicine

The WHS was not designed to look at conditions other than cardiovascular disease and cancer, so as of mid-2005, it remains an open question whether vitamin E improves immune or cognitive function or reduces cataract risk. (Vitamin E in a special formulation with vitamin C, beta carotene, and zinc has been shown to reduce the risk of advanced age-related macular degeneration.) There's also the possibility that a different aspirin-taking regimen might prevent cancer, but higher or more frequent doses of aspirin could cause greater gastrointestinal bleeding, a risk that may not be worth taking for a healthy woman.

According to study investigators and *Harvard Women's Health Watch* advisory board members Drs. I-Min Lee and JoAnn Manson, a woman's best approach to preventing heart disease and cancer is the tried-and-true combination of exercise, eating a healthy diet, weight control, not smoking, and undergoing appropriate cardiovascular health and cancer screenings.

There Is No Evidence That Shark Cartilage Fights Cancer

Janet Raloff

Janet Raloff is a senior editor at Science News.

After more than 15 years of research and various clinical trials, there still remains no evidence that shark cartilage is an effective treatment of or cure for cancer. Claims that shark cartilage will treat cancer are not only false, and misleading, but are luring people away from viable cancer treatment. Not only does this claim hurt patients, but with shark populations already at risk, perpetuating this myth is dangerous to sharks.

Shark cartilage is for sale all over the Web. Powders of it, packaged in jars and capsules, are among the products offered at sites specializing in herbal remedies, vitamins, health wares, and bodybuilding aids. These Internet sites claim that the cartilage skeletons of sharks and their close relatives—skates and rays—offer various health benefits. Inhibiting cancer is often at the top of the list. To support that contention, sellers point to studies indicating that something in shark cartilage can inhibit the blood vessel growth that tumors rely on for access to nutrients.

The idea that cancer patients who aren't helped by conventional medicine might benefit from ground-up shark skeletons was the central thesis of two books coauthored in the 1990s by nutritionist I. William Lane. Their titles argue that "sharks don't get cancer."

A *60 Minutes* television profile of Lane more than a decade ago publicized the controversial cancer treatment. Among business ventures capitalizing on the early interest was Lane Labs of Allendale, N.J. That company was created by Andrew Lane, I. William Lane's son, to sell BeneFin, a shark-cartilage product.

Several major ... studies have ... failed to show any cancer benefit in people from powdered shark cartilage.

However, shark-cartilage therapy, a large segment of the food-supplements industry, is based on severely flawed premises, according to some scientists.

A new report by one group of them contradicts the view that sharks don't get cancer. Several major recent and ongoing studies have also failed to show any cancer benefit in people from powdered shark cartilage, although a few studies report promise in a mix of chemicals extracted from cartilage as a potential anticancer pharmaceutical.

Even if current cartilage therapy isn't directly harmful, many clinicians worry that its promotion also encourages patients to give up on proven or potentially more-useful therapies.

Sharks and Cancer

The claim that sharks in the wild never get cancer first made some people conclude that something in sharks fights the disease. Yet in 1915, scientists reported a spiny dogfish shark from the Straits of Georgia sporting a thyroid tumor. In 1971, researchers described a sandbar shark caught off of Florida that had both a lymphoma and a metastatic adenocarcinoma. Reports of other shark tumors afflicting nervous, digestive, excretory, blood, reproductive, skeletal, endocrine, and skin tissues—and even cartilage—are on file at a national archive devoted to cancer in cold-blooded animals.

Gary K. Ostrander is both a marine scientist and a cancer biologist at Johns Hopkins University in Baltimore. In the

Dec. 1, 2004 *Cancer Research*, his team reviews cases of illness in captured sharks and related fish that had been filed with the Registry of Tumors in Lower Animals in Sterling, Va. The team turned up 42 cases affecting 21 species.

Forty-two tumors may not be many, Ostrander acknowledges. However, he points out, sick fish usually don't show up on hooks or in trawlers' nets. They tend to fall prey to healthy fish or just sink to the bottom, where they die of their illnesses. Therefore, he argues, "we wouldn't really expect to see many cancers," especially given that these fish normally cruise in deep waters far from shore.

Carl A. Luer of the Mote Marine Laboratory in Sarasota, Fla., doesn't buy Ostrander's argument. Many sharks and their relatives "are collected either for science or the fishing industry" he observes, "and you don't find the incidence of cancer in them that you see in bony fish."

Also, Luer failed to induce cancer in sharks during 10 years of trying to create an animal model for the human disease. For instance, he showed that the human carcinogen aflatoxin B1, which readily triggers malignancies in fish with bony skeletons, did nothing to sharks.

Even an absence of cancer in sharks ... wouldn't justify using unrefined shark cartilage as a therapy against human cancer.

Indeed, Luer tells *Science News*, "We were not able to produce anything approaching even a [precancerous] change in sharks."

Adds Robert E. Hueter, director of shark research at the Mote lab, "I've been working with sharks for 30 years, and when you see one in the wild, it tends to be very clean [of disease] when compared to other kinds of marine vertebrates, such as bony fish. Sharks also heal up quickly from any wound—and you hardly ever see a shark that looks old."

But even an absence of cancer in sharks, Hueter readily adds, wouldn't justify using unrefined shark cartilage as a therapy against human cancer.

Harvesting Shark Cartilage

If people enthusiastic about swallowing shark cartilage saw how it's harvested, they might think twice. Vessels that catch the sharks often hold the carcasses for days to weeks without refrigeration.

Some researchers doubt whether material collected in this way could maintain pharmaceutically useful properties. Because the cartilage undergoes so much decay, Hueter says, "it's just ridiculous to think it might still retain biological activity."

It certainly didn't show anticancer activity in the first major trial of powdered cartilage, conducted by Denis R. Miller, at the Cancer Treatment Research Foundation in Arlington Heights, Ill.

"We had found that a lot of patients, when we asked about their nutritional histories and use of alternative, complementary medicine, said they were taking shark cartilage," Miller notes. So, the foundation funded a study of the supplement's safety and potential efficacy in adults whose cancers of the breast, colon, rectum, prostate, lung, or other organ were not responding to conventional therapies. All participants received the recommended dose of a commercially available product called Cartilade.

Although Miller's group had planned to treat 100 people, recruitment proved difficult. However, by the time that it had 60 participants, a clear trend had emerged, says Miller, now senior director of oncology at Johnson & Johnson Pharmaceutical Research & Development in Raritan, N.J.

"We found no toxicity, but we also didn't find any benefits in tumor response," he recalls. So, his team shut down the study and published its findings in 1998.

More recently, Charles L. Loprinzi's group at the Mayo Clinic in Rochester, Minn., headed a National Cancer Institute–funded, multicenter trial comparing BeneFin and a placebo. This experiment, too, stopped early, after enrolling only about 80 of an initially planned 600 patients with intractable breast or colorectal cancer.

The limited results showed "no suggestion of a [survival] benefit and no evidence of a positive impact on quality of life" from shark cartilage, the researchers reported in New York City at the November 2004 meeting of the Society of Integrative Oncology. Moreover, they noted, by the end of a month, half of the people assigned to the cartilage regimen refused to take the more-than-1-cup daily dose.

Deterring compliance, the researchers noted, was not only the huge dose but also the product's "very fishy smell that you could detect across the room."

Becoming a Drug

The strongest evidence that shark cartilage might fight cancer comes from demonstrations that some of its components can stop the growth of new blood vessels. A tumor lures blood vessels to form on its expanding periphery, providing the pipelines to nourish it. Without this extra blood supply, a tumor can't grow.

Several anticancer drugs introduced in the past few years inhibit that process, called angiogenesis. Research by Luer and others has shown that something in fresh cartilage can block angiogenesis. That finding has spurred efforts to isolate the active components with the goal of eventually synthesizing drugs to emulate them. A major trial of the shark-derived components in patients is now under way, supported in part by Aeterna Zentaris, a pharmaceutical company headquartered in Quebec.

Its experimental drug, called Neovastat, is "not like the powdered cartilage that you find in health food stores," explains company spokesman Paul Burroughs. Although the chemistry of its antiangiogenic agents has not been characterized, he says, "we have established a standardized and well-controlled extraction of these materials from the cartilage of spiny dogfish sharks."

Laboratory tests have shown that Neovastat not only prevents blood vessel growth in tumors but also has other potentially anticancer activities, Burroughs says. For instance, the extract triggers suicide in cancer cells and inhibits enzymes that normally break down tissue around tumors, a process that can permit cancers to spread.

In a trial [in 2003] against metastatic kidney cancer, however, Neovastat failed to prolong survival of patients.

The claim that shark cartilage has medical value may further threaten already-dwindling shark populations.

Recently, the National Cancer Institute commissioned Charles Lu, an oncologist at the University of Texas–M.D. Anderson Cancer Center in Houston, to spearhead a new trial of Neovastat against recalcitrant lung cancer. The participants are "people who would typically live for, on average, up to a year and a half," Lu says. All participants will receive either Neovastat or a placebo while continuing to get radiation treatments and chemotherapy.

The 340 patients that the project has enrolled to date represent about half the number that the researchers intend to recruit. A study of that size is large enough "to have the statistical power to tease out any survival benefit" from the cartilage derivative, Lu says.

"We're doing this study because we think that addressing whether there's something special in cartilage—from a shark or any other animal—is important," Lu told *Science News.*

Federal Crackdown

Despite the absence of clear evidence that powdered shark cartilage shuts down angiogenesis, some companies are claiming that their products do just that. Recently, the Web site of Heritage Health Products of Fort Collins, Colo., stated, "Shark cartilage has been proven as an anti-angiogenic agent, as it literally starves a tumor of its blood supply [and] can prove very effective in counteracting . . . angiogenic-dependent ailments."

Making such health claims has gotten Heritage Health and other cartilage promoters in hot water.

Moves against Lane Labs began in 1997, when the Food and Drug Administration [FDA] acquired an injunction against the company and its president for the deceptive marketing of three products, including BeneFin. Although Lane Labs claimed that all three were dietary supplements or cosmetics, FDA noted that the company "promoted those products for the treatment of cancer." Such claims rendered the products drugs, the FDA charged.

The agency also cited statements by I. William Lane, a paid consultant to the company, that these products were intended for treating or preventing disease. FDA ordered Lane Labs to pull such claims from all its promotional activities.

When FDA found that the company wasn't complying, the Federal Trade Commission stepped in. In June 2000, it announced that it was fining Lane Labs $1 million for illegal activities.

Still, the case lingers. On July 9, 2004, a U.S. District Court ruled that Lane must end all U.S. distribution of the three products, unless they gain FDA approval as drugs, reimburse all buyers for those products purchased after Sept. 22, 1999, and destroy remaining stocks of the products.

Neither Lane nor any spokesperson for the company could be reached for comment. However, Marc S. Ullman, a New York City attorney whose firm was formerly retained by Lane Labs, told *Science News* that the court has stayed its call for financial outlays by the company. He added that Lane Labs has indicated that it "intends to comply with all [remaining] orders of the court." Currently, BeneFin appears to be available only via Internet dietary supplements dealers.

[In 2004], FDA began challenging the marketing of other shark-cartilage products, such as those from Heritage Health.

Other Fallout

The claim that shark cartilage has medical value may further threaten already-dwindling shark populations. Manufacturers of cartilage products favor sharks because they're much richer sources of this material than are mammals, which develop cartilage primarily in their joints, observes Merry Camhi of Islip, N.Y., a member of the shark-study group of the International Union for the Conservation of Nature and Natural Resources in Gland, Switzerland.

This focus on sharks is a problem, she and other biologists argue, because these fish are already beleaguered by the demand for their fins and, to a lesser extent, for their meat. Indeed, a Jan. 29 [2005] study in *Philosophical Transactions of the Royal Society of London: Biological Sciences* reports dramatic declines in large predatory fishes, especially sharks, during the past half century. For instance, shark populations in the North Atlantic and the Gulf of Mexico may now represent just 1 or 2 percent of their abundance 50 to 100 years ago, according to the report, which was written by Ransom A. Myers of Dalhousie University in Halifax, Nova Scotia, and Boris Worm of the Institute for Marine Science in Kiel, Germany.

Several years ago, Camhi analyzed the impact of the cartilage industry on shark populations. She concluded that the market for cartilage "makes [shark fishing] that much more lucrative" and increases pressure on populations of these fish.

This shark trade might be acceptable, Ostrander says, if cartilage therapy actually saved lives. However, he laments, after some 15 years of exploring the concept and conducting several well-controlled trials, scientists have zero evidence that it does.

Organizations to Contact

Alternative Medicine Foundation
PO Box 60016, Potomac, MD   20859-0016
(301) 340-1960
amfi@amfoundation.org
www.amfoundation.org

The Alternative Medicine Foundation is a nonprofit organization founded in March 1998 to provide responsible and reliable information about alternative medical treatment to the public and health professionals. The foundation supports traditional Chinese and Tibetan herbal formulas, acupuncture, ayurveda mind-body therapy, and other treatments as ethical alternatives to standard care and promotes novel ways of combining indigenous treatments and modern medical science. The Web site offers a wide variety of Information Resource Guides and updated research reports.

American Cancer Society (ACS)
1599 Clifton Rd. NE, Atlanta, GA   30329
(404) 320-3333
www.cancer.org

Founded in 1913, the American Cancer Society is the primary nationwide community-based voluntary organization dedicated to eliminating cancer as a major health problem through research, education, advocacy, and service. More than 3,400 local ACS offices sponsor school-based education programs, support groups, and antismoking and screening campaigns. The ACS Web site posts news of cancer conferences and meetings; maintains links to cancer-related press releases, medical updates, and exposés of cancer treatment hoaxes and myths; and offers books and kits for sale through the ACS online bookstore.

American Institute for Cancer Research (AICR)

1759 R St. NW, Washington, DC 20009
(202) 328-7744
aicrweb@aicr.org
www.aicr.org

The institute is a nonprofit research center with a focus on diet and cancer prevention. It offers educational materials to the general public and a newsletter geared toward children. Many of its publications are available online.

American Society of Clinical Oncology (ASCO)

1900 Duke St., Suite 200, Alexandria, VA 22314
(703) 299-0150
asco@asco.org
www.asco.org

ASCO Online includes information for both health professionals and people living with cancer. The society provides up-to-date information on cancer research and investigational treatment, and a calendar of events and meetings around the United States.

Cancer Research and Prevention Foundation (CRPF)

1600 Duke St., Suite 500, Alexandria, VA 22314
(703) 836-4412
info@preventcancer.org
www. preventcancer.org

Since 1985 CRPF has provided more than $74 million in support of cancer prevention research, education, and outreach programs nationwide. It continues to fund ongoing research and scientific scholarships and grants. CRPF also produces programs for local communities to help educate the public on various aspects of cancer and cancer prevention. The CRPF Web site offers links to the latest cancer research.

Cancer Research Institute

682 Fifth Ave., New York, NY   10022
(800) 99CANCER
info@cancerresearch.org
www.cancerresearch.org

The institute is a nonprofit organization that advocates, promotes, and sponsors research into cancer immunology. CRI provides information to the public and scientists on ongoing research and progress in the field of immunology. Its Web site provides archives of new reports, publications, and links to research and clinical cancer trials.

Cancer Tutor: Alternative Cancer Treatments Information Center

cancertutors@yahoo.com
www.cancertutor.com

A clearinghouse of information on alternative and natural treatments for all types and stages of cancer, *Cancer Tutor* provides links to articles and Web pages with detailed information on unorthodox treatments sometimes sought by and offered to people with advanced-stage cancers that have not responded to conventional medical treatment.

Leukemia and Lymphoma Society

1311 Mamaroneck Ave., White Plains, NY   10605
(914) 949-5213
www.leukemia-lymphoma.org

The society is the world's largest voluntary health organization dedicated to funding blood cancer research, education, and patient services. The society's mission is to find a cure for leukemia, lymphoma, Hodgkin's disease, and myeloma, and improve the quality of life of patients and their families. Its Web site provides information on diagnosis and treatment of these cancers and reviews of medical research, as well as patient resources.

Ludwig Institute for Cancer

605 Third Ave., New York, NY   10158
(212) 450-1500
www.licr.org

A global nonprofit organization dedicated to improved treatment and control of cancer. The institute actively sponsors various research projects and clinical trials.

National Breast Cancer Coalition (NBCC)

1101 17th St. NW, Suite 1300, Washington, DC 20036
(202) 296-7477 • fax: (202) 265-6854
www.natlbcc.org

The National Breast Cancer Coalition is the nation's largest breast cancer advocacy group. The goal of NBCC and its sister organization, the National Breast Cancer Coalition Fund, is to enable women to make informed, knowledgeable decisions about their own breast cancer treatments and to train members to work with legislative, scientific, and clinical decision makers in the interest of improved research and care. The Web site provides information on meetings, public policy, NBCC advocacy programs, and training.

National Cancer Institute (NCI)

NCI Public Inquiries Office, Bethesda, MD   20892
(800) 422-6237
www.cancer.gov

NCI is an arm of the federal National Institutes of Health. Established in 1937 as the principal federal agency for cancer research and training, NCI coordinates university- and hospital-based research programs as well as conducts its own cancer research. It issues the newsletter *NCI Cancer Bulletin* and the Web site offers a comprehensive archive of publications on cancer types, trends, treatment, clinical trials, genetics, and prevention.

National Center for Complementary and Alternative Medicine (NCCAM)

National Institutes of Health, 9000 Rockville Pike
Bethesda, MD   20892
(888) 644-6226
info@nccam.nih.gov
http://nccam.nih.gov

NCCAM, an agency of the federal National Institutes of Health, provides information on alternative methods of treatment for all types of disease including cancer. It supports research into alternative medicine and offers information to the general public and cancer patients about the integration of alternative treatments with conventional medicine.

Richard A. Bloch Cancer Foundation

One H&R Block Way, Kansas City, MO   64105
(816) 854-5050
www.blochcancer.org/

The foundation, founded by cancer survivor R.A. Bloch, supports cancer patients in line with its motto "Knowledge heals, ignorance destroys." The Web site offers scientific reports, informational articles for both patients and caregivers, and links to resources.

World Health Organization (WHO)

Department of Chronic Diseases and Health Promotion
Regional Office for the Americas
525 23rd St. NW, Washington, DC   20037
(202) 974-3000 • fax: (202) 974-3663
postmaster@paho.org
www.who.int/cancer/en/

WHO is the United Nations' specialized agency for health. Established in 1948, WHO tracks the incidence and distribution of disease and sponsors public health programs, education, and research aimed at improving global human health worldwide. Its Cancer Program focuses on early detection, cost-effective treatment, and prevention strategies (primarily for skin, cervical, breast, and lung cancers), well explained in a useful set of modules and research tools offered at the Web site.

Bibliography

Books

Barry Boyd and Marian Betancourt — *The Cancer Recovery Plan: How to Increase the Effectiveness of Your Treatment and Live a Fuller, Healthier Life*. New York: Penguin, 2005.

Glenn J. Bubley and Winifred Conkling — *What Your Doctor May Not Tell You About Prostate Cancer: The Breakthrough Information and Treatments That Can Help Save Your Life*. New York: Warner, 2005.

Deutsches Krebsforschungszentrum, ed. — *Current Cancer Research 2006*. Darmstadt, Germany: Steinkopff-Verlag Darmstadt, 2006.

Katrina Ellis — *Shattering the Cancer Myth: A Unique Positive Guide to Cancer Treatment Using Traditional and Natural Therapies*. Heatherton, Australia: Hinkler, 2004.

Andrea R. Genazzani — *Hormone Replacement Therapy and the Brain*. Controversial Issues in Climacteric Medicine Series. New York: Parthenon, 2003.

Kelly K. Hunt, Stephan A. Vorburger, and Stephen G. Swisher — *Gene Therapy for Cancer*. Cancer Drug Discovery and Development Series. Totowa, NJ: Humana, 2006.

Panos G. Koutrouvelis	*A Breakthrough in Prostate Cancer Treatment: What Every Man Should Know.* Vienna, VA: URPI Press, 2006.
John R. Lee, Virginia Hopkins, and David Zava	*What Your Doctor May Not Tell You About Breast Cancer: How Hormone Balance Can Help Save Your Life.* New York: Warner, 2005.
J.A. Lopez-Guerrero, A. Llombart-Bosch, and V. Felipo	*New Trends in Cancer for the 21st Century.* Advances in Experimental Medicine and Biology Series. New York: Springer, 2006.
Marc S. Micozzi, ed.	*Complementary and Integrative Medicine in Cancer Care and Prevention: Foundations and Evidence-Based Interventions.* New York: Springer, 2006.
Marion Morra and Eve Potts	*Choices: The Most Complete Sourcebook for Cancer Information.* 4th ed. New York: HarperCollins, 2003.
Michael Murray, with Tim Birdsall and Joseph E. Pizzorno	*How to Prevent and Treat Cancer with Natural Medicine.* New York: Riverhead, 2003.
National Cancer Policy Board	*Saving Women's Lives: Strategies for Improving Breast Cancer Detection and Diagnosis: A Breast Cancer Research Foundation and Institute of Medicine Symposium.* Washington, DC: National Academies Press, 2005.

Patrick Quillan — *Beating Cancer with Nutrition: Combining the Best of Science and Nature for Full Spectrum Healing in the 21st Century*. Tulsa: Nutrition Times Press, 2005.

Azzam F.G. Taktak and Anthony C. Fisher, eds. — *Outcome Prediction in Cancer*. San Diego: Elsevier, 2006.

George F. Vande Woude and George Klein, eds. — *Advances in Cancer Research*. San Diego: Elsevier, 2005.

Andrew P. Yao, ed. — *New Developments in Breast Cancer Research*. Hauppauge, NY: Nova Science, 2006.

Periodicals

Biotech Equipment Update — "Clinical Trial Tests Ultrasound Waves on Prostate Cancer," vol. 14, no. 7, July 1, 2006.

Emerging Food R&D Report — "Eating Soy May Reduce Risk of Certain Cancers," vol. 17, no. 3, June 2006.

Elizabeth Mechcatie — "FDA Waves HPV Vaccine Through," *OB GYN News*, vol. 41, no. 2, June 15, 2006.

Medical Device Week — "BrainLAB Unveils iPlan Software or 'Holistic' Cancer Treatment," June 8, 2006.

Medical Ethics Advisor — "When Minors Choose Risky, Alternative Therapies," July 1, 2006.

Web Sites

Cancer News on the Net (www.cancernews.com). A free site
dedicated to collecting the latest news and updates on
cancer prevention, research, and treatment. Overseen by a
board of medical professionals, Cancer News offers material of use to students as well as health-care providers,
cancer profile and treatment options, and information on
cancer resources. An online newsletter is available to registered users.

National Alliance of Breast Cancer Organizations (www.nabco
.org). An in-depth site providing information on all as-
pects of breast cancer. The latest treatments and research,
new drugs, support group information, and breast cancer
awareness information are all available. Supported by major breast cancer organizations to raise awareness on
breast cancer and to serve as a general resource for cancer
patients and others interested in breast cancer research.

Index